First Stories
for Thinking

ROBERT FISHER

Nash Pollock
Publishing

© 1999 Robert Fisher

First published in 1999 by
Nash Pollock Publishing
32 Warwick Street
Oxford OX4 1SX

9 8 7 6

Orders to:
York Publishing Services
64 Hallfield Road
Layerthorpe
York YO31 7ZQ

A catalogue record of this book is available from the British
Library.

ISBN 1 898255 29 6

Design, typesetting and production management by
Black Dog Design, Buckingham

Printed in Great Britain by The Cromwell Press, Wiltshire.

Contents

Appendices

Introduction

'What's the point of a story unless you think about it?'
                                    Karen, aged six

First Stories for Thinking is a resource aimed at developing the thinking, learning and literacy skills of young children. It offers thirty multi-cultural stories for children aged 4-8 years to enjoy and to think about. Each story is followed by a discussion plan of questions to challenge and extend children's thinking about the story, and a discussion plan that focuses on a major theme from it. Follow-up activities are suggested to encourage children to develop literacy skills and to extend their understanding.

The stories and discussion plans can be used in a variety of ways, including as part of a Literacy Hour lesson, and as a stimulus for thinking with individual children, small groups, whole classes or with larger groups of children such as a school assembly.

The stories may be read for their own sake by the teacher or child or groups of children, and used to stimulate thinking and discussion. Included are stories from a range of cultures, including folktales from Africa, China, Europe, India and the West Indies. The stories provide an ideal context for developing speaking, listening, and response to literature.

First Stories for Thinking can be used for developing a community of enquiry in the classroom, through questioning and discussion, reading, writing, and other creative activities such as art and drama, to help develop thinking and philosophy for children.

Why read stories?

'A story is something that might happen to you'
                                    Anne, aged seven

A story can provide a young child with their greatest mental challenge. A good story presents to the child a possible world as an object of intellectual enquiry. Stories that have stood the test of time do so because they inspire curiosity and contain many layers of meaning. The deeper meanings of stories may reveal themselves only after many readings, or after being discussed and interpreted with others. Stories also offer metaphors for life. When we begin 'Once upon a time …' the story might be about ourselves, for our lives can also be seen as narratives bound by time and space. Any story might also be our story. It might, as Anne said, happen to you.

What children gain from reading stories hardly needs spelling out. Hearing or reading a story expands the mind, and allows children to enter new worlds and to lead other lives. These benefits may also be gained by watching a story unfold on television or film. So what is special about *reading* a story?

What makes reading special is that language is a more demanding medium than film or TV. Pictures look like what they represent. Words printed on a page do not. They are black marks. A child, struggling with reading, when asked why reading was difficult replied: 'It's hard because words don't show you what they mean.' A young child when asked what a word was said: 'It's made up of kind of squiggly things, like tadpoles.' Words appear as a swarm of black marks on paper. If the written code is to mean anything it has to be deciphered, and although skilled readers do it instantly, the ability to translate printed words into spoken words is an amazingly complex operation.

The first challenge a reader must face is to break the code, and find an answer to the question: *What does it say?* A written text provides a stimulus for code-breaking. To follow the story we need to do more than say the words, we must make meaning from words. A reader of or listener to stories has to be a meaning-maker, seeking answers to the question: *What does it mean?* In so doing the reader must invoke a kind of imaginative power, different from other mental processes. The ability to translate words into mental images helps us to give meaning to a story.

This book differs from other kinds of story books in that it contains no pictures. Stories without pictures encourage the reader or listener to translate the words into visual images, and make a creative response by opening up the possibility of many different interpretations. They stimulate visual thinking and invite children to conjure up their own mental pictures to create a theatre of the mind. When there are pictures, whether as illustrations in a book, or as images in a film, the meaning is fixed. Words without pictures challenge the reader to create their own images, and make their own interpretive response. As Paul, aged six, says: 'I like to see pictures in my own mind.'

Reading is not just the act of re-creating words as images in the mind. To be a critical reader means to be able to make a personal response to the story, to seek answers to the question: *What does it mean to me?* This is a creative act, for no story or page will be responded to in quite the same way by any two readers. The reader is not the 'author' of the text, as some theorists have claimed, any more than a pianist playing Mozart is Mozart. But a reader, like a musician, is engaged in an act of interpretation which is also an act of self expression. We can play a piece of music or read a story at a literal level by playing the notes or reading the words. But at a deeper level we understand the story (or music) by linking it to our own experience of life. This provides the deeper pleasures in reading, and explains why we can go back to the same story or book and gain pleasure from reading it again and again. As Tracy, aged eight, put it: 'A good story makes you think, how would you feel if it happened to you.'

A story becomes humanly rewarding when we respond to it. Without some emotional engagement or personal response, reading a story becomes a mere exercise. Real reading takes mental effort. As Tom, aged six, says: 'Reading a book is more tiring than playing a game of football.' Reading a story, and then discussing it with others, can be both the most tiring, challenging and exhilarating of activities. This also helps explain why seeing a story you know on television can be so disappointing. It is disappointing because part of the creative activity has been done for you, and in a way that may not correspond to your own conception of the story or its characters. The pictures beam into the visual part of the brain, and you need to do little or no work for yourself, for what you supply to a story through the act of reading has been left out. As with a picture book or comic, telling a story in pictures rather than words can provide the child with a rich visual or narrative experience, but it is a different experience from reading or listening to a story.

Finally, if children are to become critical readers in the fullest sense they also need to be reading-users, and to answer the question: *What can we do with it?* Critical readers are able to re-create and respond to texts, and also to use them for their own creative purposes. Any story can be a stimulus for their own story-writing. Questions that encourage the re-creating of texts include: What happened next? What might have been a different ending to the story? Can you write or tell your own version of the story? Can you write a similar kind of story? Can you act, draw or paint a scene from the story, or make music to accompany the story? Can you use the story for different purposes or audiences, for example writing it as a news story, using it as a stimulus for research or making it into a board game?

A good story draws us in by engaging the emotions. Rahim, aged six, explained this by saying: 'In a good story you never know what is going to happen next.' This is one of many cognitive challenges offered a story. A good story requires good thinking. How then do we use stories to develop good thinking and so help children become critical and skilled readers?

Adventures in thinking

'What does the story mean?'

Holly, aged seven

'A good story is adventure,' said Ben, aged six. It is an adventure for the characters involved, but is also an adventure in thinking. It invites the reader to make a leap of imagination. We need to help children to make that leap and expand their thinking. One way of doing this is through questioning. By asking questions we model what good readers do as they try to make sense of what they read. We ask the questions we hope our children will later learn to ask themselves. Such questions help develop the habits of mind of good readers. They practise with us what they will later do by themselves. So what kinds of question should we be asking?

A story has a setting, so one question we can always ask is: *What kind of world is this?* All stories occur in a place and at some time. Part of the adventure of a story is to be taken on a magic carpet of the mind to other places and other times, to meet other people doing things that might be very similar or very different to what we do. We can explore the world of any story by asking questions such as:

- *Setting*   When is it (now or a long time ago)?

  Where is it (here or somewhere else)?

  What is it like there (how is it like/unlike here)?

- *Character*   Who are the characters in the story (can you name them)?

- *Plot*

How would you describe them (what do they look like)?

How are the characters related?

What happens in the story?

What was/were the key events?

What might have happened?

- *Point of view*

What does the character think?

What do the other characters think?

What do you think?

- *Dialogue*

What did the character(s) say?

Why did they say that?

What might they have said?

- *Language*

What special words are there (what new words)?

What sound/spelling patterns can you see?

What punctuation is used? Why?

- *Themes*

What is the story about?

What is strange, interesting or puzzling about the story?

What questions or comments do you have about the story?

After reading or hearing the story, the first challenge we can present to a young child is to ask them to recollect and retell the events of the story in their own words. Young children are of course very keen to tell a story in the right way, in the right order. As Lucy, aged five, said after hearing some deviation in the retelling of the Cinderella story: 'That's not the right story. You have got to tell it right.'

Once the story is established in their minds, children can enjoy playing with the narrative if they are encouraged to do so. An example of this occurred when Rumpelstiltskin was being used as a story for thinking with five year olds*. Once we had read, reconstructed and discussed the story I invited some of them to act out their own version

in front of the class. They volunteered to play the different parts, and with a few props began acting the story. The child playing the king rode into the village, listened to the mother in the story say how her daughter could spin straw into gold. The king then asked whether the daughter would go with him to the palace to spin some straw into gold. The mother thought about this request and then said: 'No'. The king asked again, the daughter said she would go but the mother said no. The king tried once more but again the mother said no, her daughter could not go with the king, she must stay at home. So the king not knowing what to do 'rode' away and that was the end of their version of the story. Afterwards I asked the girl who played the mother why she had not followed the story and allowed the king to take her daughter to the palace. She replied: 'Because I knew what would happen if he did!'

Another kind of personal response is to try to visualise the setting, characters or events in the story. Some children, like adults, are better at seeing with their 'mind's eye' than others. Visual thinking is an important means of learning, remembering and coming to know things. We are all to some extent visual learners, and visual intelligence is one of the many kinds of intelligence we all need to develop†. Some children learn best through exercising their visual intelligence. One way to stimulate this capacity is to ask them to close their eyes and to visualise the story they are reading or hearing in their 'mind's eye', or take them for a walk through an imagined scene which you describe while they try to visualise what it looks like. Talk afterwards about what they could see, or not see. One child reported after a visualisation session: 'Its like you've got a telly inside your head,' but another responded: 'The trouble is I don't know how to switch mine on.'

We make a story meaningful by linking it to personal experience, and by identifying with the characters. When a group of six year olds was asked which character in the story of Cinderella they would like to be, one child replied: 'A mouse' (the sort that was changed into a horse to pull Cinderella's carriage). When asked why he said: 'Because I like cheese, and so does a mouse.' If

---

* See *Stories for Thinking*, in this series, p 91 for story and discussion plans for Rumpelstiltskin.

† See *Head Start: How to Develop Your Child's Mind* by Robert Fisher (Souvenir Press, 1999) for a discussion of a child's multiple intelligences and ways to develop them.

you were a character in the story who would you want to be? Why? What would you do, say, think and feel? Other questions that help children make personal links with a story include:

- Are there any characters in the story that seem to be like you?
- Did the story remind you of anything you have done?
- Did the story remind you of anyone you know?
- How would you feel if that happened to you?
- Would you/do you do things like that
- Who in the story would you like to be a friend of? Why?
- What do you like or not like about this story?

Young children often find it difficult to articulate a personal response to a story. As Melanie, aged seven, said: 'Its hard to say what you mean.' But although what they say can seem incoherent their insights may contain the seeds of more sophisticated understanding. They often have in their minds more than they can say. Our challenge is to help them to develop and express their understanding; to think for themselves, give voice to their thinking, form their own judgements and personal insights, and take pride in having a personal point of view. One method for achieving this, which has been used successfully across the world, is that of Philosophy for Children. This is a method of using a story as a stimulus for creating what is called a 'Community of Enquiry' with any group of children*. Before looking at ways of using stories in a community of enquiry, and as part of a Literacy Hour, we will try to identify some other key skills developed through using a 'Stories for Thinking' approach.

Developing literacy

'Oh I get it, we're not supposed to read the story, we are supposed to think about it'

James, aged seven

Once a child is able to 'crack' the language code through being able to read and write at a basic level, they will need to practise their reading with challenging texts and develop the higher order skills that will enable them extend and improve their standard of reading. The following are some of the higher order reading skills that this book aims to develop:

- skimming
- scanning
- reflective reading: questioning and analysing
- reasoning: making inferences, deductions and connections
- evaluating

Skimming is the ability to get the overall gist of a text, to gather the main points. Asking the child to skim through the story before or after you have read it and then to reconstruct it together provides practice in skimming. The ability to skim a story or book is important for quickly finding out what the writing is about. This can be done at a superficial level, like Woody Allen who, when asked what Dostoievsky's *War and Peace* was about, said 'Russia', or the child when asked to say what 'The Cats and the Chappatti' (p 56) was about said: 'A cat'. The value of short stories, as in this book, is that skimming can be done relatively easily by both adult and child. Have a quick look at one of the stories and see how quickly (and accurately) you can tell what the story is about or recall it. You can also ask children to play this 'skimming the story' game.

Scanning means looking rapidly but intensely at a text to identify a particular part such as the name of a character or when a particular event occurred. Questions to encourage children to actively scan the text include : 'Can you find the part in the story where ...' or if children are referring to the story: 'Show me where in the story it says ...'. Play games such as Hunt the Word, to help develop their scanning skills by asking them to scan the story to find a particular word, sentence or punctuation mark.

Reflective reading includes the ability to question what you read, and to be thoughtful in response to texts. This is important if children are to learn from and to evaluate what they read. A young child will learn to question by seeing others do it, and if they practise asking questions themselves. The stories in this book are there to be analysed and questioned. When asked how many questions could be asked about one of the stories, one child (aged seven) who had had much practice in asking questions about stories replied: 'More than

---

* See *Teaching Thinking: Philosophical Enquiry in the Classroom* (Cassell, 1998) by Robert Fisher for an introduction to the theory and practice of Philosophy for Children, and *Poems for Thinking* (Nash Pollock, 1997) for ways of using poems in a community of enquiry.

any of us can think of. You can never run out of questions, because there is always another question.'

Reasoning involves making inferences and deductions from text. The trouble with language is that words are not the objects they describe and represent. All words are in a sense metaphoric. They stand for things, but are not the things themselves. Therefore they are in a sense always incomplete. The words 'old woman' for example might refer to any one of a number of old women, who might be a range of ages or even of different genders! So we can always ask, 'Who is this old woman?' and 'What is she like?' and draw inferences from clues in the text to help answer the question. Inferences involve using reasons or evidence to reach a conclusion which is more or less likely to be true. During the discussion of one story, a child suggested that the woman in the story might be a man dressed up as a woman. This was of course possible, but the children decided that this was unlikely for there was no evidence in the story to support it. 'What man would want to dress up as a woman?' asked Darren (a question we decided to discuss another time).

Deductions are inferences from text using reasoning alone. For example if a character is referred to as 'she', the character must be female. This is true by definition, like other things about her, such as that if she is a person one day she was born and one day she will die. If all humans are mortal and Cinderella is human, then Cinderella must be mortal. We can deduce a lot from the meanings of words, which is why getting children to explain and define words is so important. 'It depends what you mean by ...' is a frequent question posed by philosophers, for they know that many arguments and misunderstandings in life arise because people interpret the meanings of words differently. We make inference and deductions from stories by exploring what the words of the story imply. As Jade, aged five, said, puzzling over a word she did not understand: 'If I knew what the word meant I'd know the story.'

To be a critical reader we do more than know the story. We are able to evaluate the story and can compare it with other stories. Evaluating means critically assessing the story, by judging for example what we like or do not like about a story, what is good or not good about it. One way to evaluate a story is to compare it with others that we know or have read, for every good story:

- has an author (or number of authors)
  Who is telling this story?

- is a special kind of story (genre)
  What kind of story is this?

- can be linked to other stories
  Is this like another story you know? How?

- is special (or original in some way)
  What is special about this story?

Stories and moral development

'Thinking can help you be a better person'

Kirandeep, aged eight

All the stories in this book have a moral dimension. They are therefore suitable for reading in a school assembly or on other occasions when a stimulus for moral thinking is needed. Each story explores some aspects of moral behaviour.

We often find it easier to understand fictional situations than situations in our own lives, because stories about others can be viewed from a more dispassionate viewpoint. The challenging aspects of life are less threatening in stories than in real life. Stories are therefore an excellent vehicle for discussing moral issues, initiating children into thinking about meanings and values, through asking questions such as:

How are people (characters) behaving in the story?

How should they behave?

How would you behave if you were them?

Other questions that can help children to explore the moral dimensions of any story include:

Key question	Moral dimension
'Have we thought of...'	Imagination
'How would you feel if...?'	Empathy
'What if everybody did...?'	Universalising a principle
'What would happen if...?'	Anticipating consequences
'What alternatives are there...?'	Hypothetical reasoning
'Is it a good reason...?'	Giving good reasons
'Is this the sort of person you want to be?'	Projecting an ideal self
'Is this the sort of world you'd like to live in?'	Projecting an ideal world

One of the best ways to involve children in developing literacy and the exercise of moral judgement through the use of story is by creating a community of enquiry. A community of enquiry is a community that teaches by example, enabling children to practise the sorts of reasonable behaviour we hope they will develop as everyday habits of mind. It gives them the experience of being in a group where being reasonable (that is, giving reasons for what you say and do) and listening to others, is the norm. By encouraging children to think, reason and make moral judgements about the behaviour of others, they are likely to become more reasonable and thoughtful about their own behaviour. As Liane, aged seven, said, in summing up what she learnt from a thinking story: 'You should always stop and think first.'

Creating a Community of Enquiry

'You should listen to other people because sometimes they have good ideas'

Jamie, aged six

A community of enquiry is a place where you share a story, and discuss it in a safe and stimulating environment, where children think for themselves and learn to value the thinking of others.

If young children are going to share their thoughts and feelings they must feel safe to do so. When children take the risk of revealing their thoughts they become very vulnerable. The first task in a community of enquiry is to make children feel comfortable, secure and at ease with their teacher and with each other. Ideally adult and child should be sitting at the same level, on floor or chairs in a circle so that all can see, hear and talk to each other easily. This may not be possible; even so a sense of community can be achieved in a setting which is not ideal.

Try not to be interrupted. There is important learning going on. This is not any kind of 'storytime' activity, but an attempt to engage children in the most challenging kinds of thinking and discussion. It should take priority, if possible, over whatever might interrupt the concentration of the children. To avoid disturbance one teacher puts a sign outside her class saying: 'Do not disturb, thinking in progress.'

In a community of enquiry the teacher takes responsibility for creating the *form* of the discussion, but the *content* should be as far as possible the responsibility of the children. As with any discussion certain ground rules may need to be established, for example: 'We take turns, we speak one at a time, we listen to each other, and we respect what people say.' It can be helpful to talk about what the rules should be beforehand, and to write them up (in words or pictures) for all to see. A four year old once said he 'hated school' (meaning his nursery class). When asked why, he said: ' 'Cos no-one listens to me'. A community of enquiry is a place where everyone is listened to, and where everyone has a chance to say what they think.

It can be helpful to begin by playing some simple games that embody the rules of the community of enquiry*. 'Throw and Say' for example is a good game to play with young children. They sit in a circle and gently throw a beanbag or soft ball randomly to each other in turn. Whoever holds the ball tells the rest of the group about their weekend experiences. No one is allowed to interrupt the speaker. When each has had a turn the ball is thrown back to the teacher. An advantage of this game is that it gives every child a chance to speak, and ensures that everyone listens.

Children who engage in a community of enquiry acquire habits which reflect their experience in the community. If they listen to each other, express their own opinions, and build on each other's ideas they will grow into children who are willing to listen, who are confident in saying what they think and who are thoughtful about what others say. They also grow in confidence and self esteem.

So how is a community of enquiry created? In a typical community of enquiry the teacher will:
- read the story
- invite comments or questions
- lead a discussion
- invite children to review the discussion
- introduce some further activity.

---

* See *Games for Thinking* (Nash Pollock, 1997) in this series for some thinking games for seven year olds and over that can be adapted for use with young children.

This is how these elements apply to a Stories for Thinking lesson:

1 Reading the story

If the children are non-readers the teacher will read or tell the story. It is helpful with young children to read the story twice. The second time is a 'thinking time' when as they listen they are asked to think about anything that might be strange, interesting or puzzling about the story. When children can read, the readers take turns in reading part of the story (usually a paragraph each). Any children in the group who cannot read or who find reading very difficult say 'pass', and the next child continues the reading.

In a community of enquiry everyone has the right to a voice and a vote. They may wish to suggest different ways of approaching the story. The thinking circle is a natural setting in which to explore not only stories but issues of personal concern. As Justin, aged eight, put it: 'I like our philosophy sessions because you don't have to just think of the story, you can talk about what is important as well.'

2 Inviting comments or questions

'You see things and ask "Why?"
But I dream things that never were; and I say "Why not?"' George Bernard Shaw

'I have a lot of questions that I haven't yet thought of.' Cassie, aged seven

After the story has been read by teacher and children, it is time to think about the story. Allow some quiet thinking time, then ask the children if there is anything strange, interesting or puzzling about the story. Prevent quick children (the 'hare brains' in the group) from shouting out the first thing they think of by saying you are going to give everyone time to think. Building in 'thinking time' will help children have more ideas (particularly those 'tortoise minds' who think slower but perhaps no less well than the 'hare brains'). Thinking time will also encourage more thoughtful responses, more elaborate thinking and better questions.

Once they have had time to think, ask for their comments or questions, and write each one in the child's words on the board. Add the child's name after their comment or question to acknowledge each contribution. You may need to help the child

to formulate their comment into a question or to fully express their thought. Try as much as possible to use the child's own words, and check with them that the changes you propose are what they want to say – as in the following excerpt from discussion:

Child	He was a bad man.
Teacher	We could turn that into a question, couldn't we – 'Was he a bad man?' or 'Why was he a bad man?'
Child	Why was he a bad man. (Teacher now writes this up as a question.)

Once you have a number of questions or comments on the board, each linked to the name of one or more children (for several children might have the same thought or idea) you will have a number of responses to the story to explore in discussion. Choose one of the questions, or ask the children to choose a question by voting which one they would like to discuss. When the question has been chosen, begin the discussion by asking the child whose question it is to say why they asked the question, and invite others to respond to what is said.

One advantage of writing questions on a board (or large piece of paper) is that you have a record of contributions that can be added to later, or compared with other lists. A frequent finding is that the more experienced children become at interrogating texts the better they at it they are. As one teacher reports: 'For the first few stories the children gave few comments or questions, after six weeks I got twice as many, and now (after a term) they often ask more questions than I can fit onto the board.' Of her lists of questions another teacher said: 'It provides me with written evidence that this is an enquiring classroom.'

3 Leading a discussion

'I like it when we have a "thinking time" about stories'

Sonal, aged six

One way to facilitate the discussion is to ask who agrees or disagrees with particular comments that have been made. The aim of the teacher is to lead but not to dominate the discussion. Initially you will need to ask a lot of questions yourself, particularly the key question: 'Why?' As the group gets better at discussing together, the balance of teacher and pupil participation should change. As a community develops the children should do more of the speaking. As Jemma, aged eight, said:

'A story circle is different because it is our turn to say what we think.'

The following is part of a discussion with Year 2 children after they had read 'The Cats and the Chapatti' (p 56). They had chosen to answer Anna's question about the story: 'Why did they quarrel?'

Child	There were some animals quarrelling.
Teacher	What were they saying?
Child	'No you can't', 'Yes you can' ... that sort of thing.
Child	They were contradicting each other.
Teacher	So a quarrel is like a contradiction?
Child	... (after a pause for thought) Yes.
Child	They were quarrelling with each other.
Teacher	Can you quarrel with yourself?
Child	You can't quarrel with yourself. You need to have more than one person.
Child	You can quarrel with yourself. You could punch yourself. Your brain quarrels with you ... if you want to test yourself.
Child	I disagree with Sarah. You can't quarrel with yourself. You haven't done anything to yourself.
Child	If you punch your leg, it can't say no. Your brain says no.
Teacher	Can animals say 'Yes' and 'No'?
Child	No, only people can say 'Yes' and 'No'. That's how we are different from animals.

At the end of the discussion the children were asked to say what they thought the moral of the story was. Here are some of their replies:

- 'Don't trust anyone' (James)
- 'Don't fight and quarrel' (Andrew)
- 'Don't be greedy or someone may take what you've got' (Ryan)
- 'Share with other people' (Conor)
- 'Don't fight or quarrel with your friends' (Sarah)
- 'Be kind to everyone' (Emily)

In the early stages of a community of enquiry, discussions tend to be totally teacher directed, but the aim is to shift the focus off yourself so that they will, through working together, become able to take more responsibility for the discussion and for the way the community of enquiry functions. Try to encourage this, once the children are

familiar with the process, by asking them to respond to each other and to look at the person to whom they are responding (not at you). Introduce the convention 'I agree with...' or 'I disagree with ...' and get the children to say who they are agreeing or disagreeing with. Sometimes invite the child who has spoken to nominate the next speaker (if there is more than one other who wishes to speak).

You would expect to see evidence of progress after a number of sessions. The sorts of evidence teachers report seeing include children being better able to:

Evidence	*Skills*
listen to each other	*listening skills*
formulate and ask questions	*questioning and enquiry skills*
think of good/new ideas	*creative thinking*
translate their thoughts and ideas into words	*communication*
communicate their ideas	*speaking skills*
respond to others in a discussion	*cooperative and social skills*
give reasons for what they think	*verbal reasoning skills*
develop their understanding of challenging concepts	*concept building*
read and critically respond to texts	*critical reading skills*

By participating in a community founded on reasoning, freedom of expression and mutual respect, the children will experience what it means to be a free citizen in a democracy and to exercise personal choice. There is no better preparation for being an active citizen in a democracy than for a child to participate with others in a community of enquiry.

Discussion plans

To aid discussion there are two sets of questions at the end of each story. These questions aim to sustain and foster a sense of wonder and curiosity about the story and about a major theme from the story.

The first set of questions challenges children's thinking at the literal level of the story, by probing their knowledge of the text and their ability to draw inferences from it. They are questions about reading the lines and 'reading between the lines'. These comprehension questions are not all the questions that could be asked about the story, nor are they there to be automatically worked through after every story. They are models for the kinds of questions you could ask if children have no questions to ask for themselves.

The second set of questions is philosophical. They ask questions about a theme or concept drawn from the story. Again these model the kinds of question you could ask about this or other themes in the story. What makes these themes, such as sharing, anger, beauty and so on, philosophical is that they are conceptual, and encourage abstract rather than literal thinking. Answers to these questions rely not on knowing things about the story (although they relate to what happens in the story), but on thinking about things in life. They are about reading beyond the lines. They seek a personal response to issues that are central to human existence, but which are open-ended, challenging and contestable. They do not seek to find one right answer, but encourage children to consider a variety of viewpoints, ideas and arguments. They are not about trying to find the right answer from other people, or about 'guessing what is in the teacher's head'. They are about saying what you think in the best possible way.

Choose from the discussion plans questions you think are appropriate and challenging for your children, and seed your own questions into the discussion. By creating your own discussion plan beforehand you will always have something to ask if the discussion flags, and by so doing you model for the child the intelligent habits of an enquiring reader.

One of the exciting aspects of a community of enquiry is its unpredictability. Whatever plan you have to lead children on through a series of questions, you never quite know where the discussion will lead or what children will say next, like the child who suddenly told the group her grandmother did not need false teeth (when asked why she replied, 'Because she's dead') or the child who stopped the flow of discussion by asking: 'Does God have a God?' You will never know for sure what the children will want to explore during a discussion, or quite where it will go. Nor will you expect to if you want children to be engaged in critical, creative and imaginative thinking.

The enquiry need not end when the discussion ends. Thinking can be extended through further activities, including allowing time to review the discussion.

4 Reviewing the discussion

'Its easier to talk than to think about what you've said'

Adam, aged seven

Leaving time to review the discussion gives time for children to think about what has been said. Questions that encourage children to remember and review the discussion include:

- 'Did we ask good questions?'
  Who remembers a good question we asked?
- 'Did we listen to each other?'
  Who remembers what we discussed?
- 'Did we have good ideas?'
  Who remembers someone who had a good idea?
- 'Did we give good reasons?'
  Who remembers someone giving a good reason?
- 'Did we have a good discussion?'
  What part of the discussion was best?

Review time should be about assessing how good the discussion was, and who contributed good ideas, and should also include opportunities for self assessment. An important element of this is to see if children can remember what they said, what ideas they had and whether they changed their minds. Any child who indicates they have changed their mind through listening to others or thinking things through should be especially praised. Some have argued that self correction is the highest form of intelligent behaviour; it is also one of the hardest and should at all times be encouraged. Remember to encourage the risk-takers, those children who have made a bold speculation, created an interesting hypothesis or expressed a novel idea.

5 Introducing further activities

'Can I draw what I think?'

Maisie, aged six

Follow-up activities enable children to focus on different aspects of the story, allowing their thinking processes to work in creative and indirect ways rather than as directed by the teacher during discussion. A drawing activity, for example, is not only useful in providing an opportunity for self-expression for a child who cannot write, it allows any child a means to make their thinking visible, shared with others and open to discussion and review. As one teacher said: 'It is not only the drawing that is important, it is getting children to look at it and talk about it that gives it value.'

An extension activity should give children the chance to look and think again about the subject. After each discussion plan there is a 'Further Activities' section with suggestions for ways of extending thinking and developing different literacy skills. The first three further activities in each list focus on three key elements of literacy, namely developing children's understanding at:

- text level
- sentence level
- word level

The Literacy Hour which has been introduced into primary schools in England and Wales stresses the importance of work with children at text, word and sentence level, and after each story there are ideas for further work at these levels in the Literacy Hour.

Stories and the Literacy Hour

'When we are talking about stories I like to have enough time to do it'

Kate, aged six

'The teacher demonstrates reading strategies with a shared text. The class reads the text together and discusses ideas and textual features, engaging in a high level of interaction with the teacher.'

(*National Literacy Strategy* definition of shared reading)

The stories in this book are ideal for use in the shared reading part of a Literacy Hour. The Literacy Hour is divided into work at text, sentence and word levels, each given an allotted amount of time - shared reading (15 mins) followed by word and sentence work (15 mins) with the whole class, independent reading and writing activities (20 mins) followed by a 10 minute plenary session for sharing work.

During shared reading the teacher demonstrates reading strategies using a shared text. As in a community of enquiry the class reads the story together, discusses ideas and textual features, engaging in a high level interaction with the teacher. The stories can also be a stimulus for group and individual reading activities. The Stories for Thinking approach can add value to a Literacy Hour through its emphasis on critical thinking, pupil questioning and reasoning. Some of the similarities and differences between Stories for Thinking, using a community of enquiry approach, and the Literacy Hour as outlined in the National Literacy Strategy, is shown in Fig 1:

A Literacy Hour	Stories for Thinking
aims to develop:	*aims to develop:*
Literacy: reading, writing, speaking and listening	Literacy: critical thinking, questioning and reasoning
Reading and reflecting at text level, with emphasis on teacher questioning	Reading and reflecting on text, with emphasis on pupil questioning
Sentence level work to improve comprehension and composition	Sentence level work in creating questions and comments
Word level work to improve phonics, spelling and vocabulary	Word level work in defining meanings of words
A plenary review for sharing and presenting work	Review of the discussion, including self assessment

Figure 1

The Literacy Hour and Stories for Thinking share some common features. Both emphasise the importance of discussing the text to identify themes, ideas, and implicit meanings. Both aim to develop critical reading skills. Stories for Thinking emphasises the importance of children formulating their own questions, and aims to add philosophical depth to the discussion. The Literacy Hour emphasises the importance of work at word and sentence level as well as text level. Suggestions for work at text, sentence and word level are included here under Further Activities at the end of each story. These activities can be done with the whole class, with groups or for individual work as part of a Literacy Hour.

The following are some activities to use with the stories at text, sentence and word level:

Text level

- Ask children to find and name all the characters in the story.
- Ask children to recall details of the story in sequence.
- Dramatise the story by adding actions or sound effects; invite a child to mime or read a character's part.
- Invite children to record the plot of the story on a map, time line, circle or ladder (see p 76).
- Ask children to compare the theme of this story with other stories they know or have read.
- Give the story a star rating e.g. * (1 star), ** (2 stars) or *** (3 stars) and say why.
- Think of another title for this story that sums up what it is all about.
- Think of a new ending to make the story funnier, happier or more exciting.
- Play Mystery Character. Choose a character. Children question you to try to find out who it is e.g. 'Where does *x* live?'
- Write instructions based on a story e.g. 'How to make a chappatti' (p 56).

Sentence level

- Identify the punctuation in a story and discuss its use e.g. 'What is a full stop for?'
- Read part of the story, making deliberate mistakes. Can the children spot each mistake?
- Ask children to identify capital letters at the start of sentences; match the letter you are holding.
- Find speech marks, rewrite some dialogue in speech bubbles linked to a picture of a character.
- Ask children to find and read a sentence. Discuss what makes it a sentence.
- Discuss what the punctuation makes voices do in reading a story e.g. full stop, comma, question, exclamation mark etc.
- Collect sentences which are questions; discuss words or phrases which begin questions e.g. who, what etc.
- Find and highlight joining words such as *then, next, after that, suddenly, meanwhile* etc.
- Start sentences for children to finish e.g. 'I like the bit when … because …'
- Ask children to add to a phrase from the story to make it into a sentence (then add a joining word to make a more complex sentence).

Word level

- Ask children to identify particular lower case letters, to match the letter you are holding.
- Ask children to identify the letters/digraphs at the beginnings of words e.g. 'ch', 'sh', 'th'.
- Show the child a long word e.g. 'goodbye'. Can they find the word within the word?
- Look for alliterative phrases e.g. 'What do you notice about "beautiful baby"?'
- Identify words that rhyme, look for rhyming patterns of letters, find new rhyming words.
- Cover a word in the text. Can the children predict what the missing word is?
- Highlight a difficult word in the text. Show a step-by-step approach to reading the word.
- Make a deliberate error in reading a word. Can children spot which word was wrong? Can they read the word?
- Brainstorm synonyms (or antonyms) for a chosen word from the text.
- Create a mind-map of words associated with a key word from the text e.g. words to describe a setting or character*.

* See *The National Literacy Strategy* (DfEE, 1998) for more on text, sentence and word level work.

Many teachers are exercising their professional judgement in adapting the Literacy Hour to benefit from of a Stories for Thinking approach. Others prefer to find time, usually once a week, for more extended story discussion than the Literacy Hour allows. *First Stories for Thinking* is a flexible resource for you to use in ways which suit you and your children. It will develop literacy but is about more than literacy, it is also about teaching children to think, in particular to think philosophically about stories and about themselves and the world. It provides an ideal introduction to doing Philosophy for Children.

Philosophy for children

'Why do things happen the way they do?'

Dawn, aged eight

'Can you tell me how the world began?
Who made the first woman and man?

Before I was born where was I?
What will happen when I die?

Where is heaven and what is hell?
Is there a God? How can you tell?

I have so many questions in my head.'
'Now then, darling, it's time for bed.'

The wonderful thing about young children is that they are natural philosophers. They want to know the meaning of things, and one of the pleasures of working with young children is that they are not afraid to ask. Some of these questions will be about everyday things: 'What is that called?' 'Why is she doing that?' 'Where is he going?' There is often a simple answer to these factual questions which is right or wrong.

Other questions that children ask will be harder to answer. These will be questions about what things mean and why life is like it is, for example: 'Why do people die?' 'Why do people hate each other?' 'What is God?' These are questions that are about human life, and how we think about life. Such questions not only puzzle children; they have been puzzling philosophers for thousands of years. They are common because we all have the capacity to ask philosophical questions. It is just that we may not do it very often, and as we get older we may stop asking these kinds of question. Children too will stop if not encouraged. As children get older they usually ask fewer questions, and some stop asking questions at all. This may be because they are discouraged from asking questions at home, or in school. If no-one is

interested then why ask questions? As Charlotte, aged 11, said, 'I stopped asking questions. Everyone seemed to know the answers except me, and no-one wanted to listen.'

One of the problems with children's questions is that sometimes there is no easy answer, or there may be a whole range of possible answers, or the answer may not be known by us or by anybody. Here are some questions asked by four and five year old children. Some are scientific in that there is a factual answer, others are the kind for which there may be no easy answer – they are philosophical:

- 'Why do hairs grow out of grandma's nose?'
- 'Where do people go when they die?'
- 'Why is it wrong to steal?'
- 'Can rabbits think?'
- 'Is magic real?'
- 'Do snails love each other?'
- 'Are there really angels?'

Philosophy for Children provides the opportunity for children to ask and to discuss questions about what is strange, interesting or puzzling about the world. It works through creating a community of philosophical enquiry with children of any age or ability, including children as young as four or five years old. The method presupposes that children are capable of discussing important issues such as right and wrong, friendship, fairness, truth, beauty, stealing and so on. These are issues not only of general human concern, but also problems that have exercised the minds of philosophers for centuries.

Young children are often good at raising questions but not good at discussing possible answers. Often this is because they lack practice. Young children tend to expect to have their questions unequivocally answered by grown-ups, not discussed by other children. They are not used to having their attention focused on a particular issue for a length of time, or to discuss something in a systematic and sustained way, or to consider things from a variety of viewpoints. But if they have a stimulus (for example a story) then even young children can respond to questions in ways that can be called pre-philosophical or philosophical. This means moving them from the concrete and literal aspects of the story to the conceptual and the abstract, moving from discussing *what* happened in the story to *why*. The discussion might be pre-philosophical when seeking some kind of explanation, and it becomes philosophical when it is about a general concept such as truth or beauty.

Discussion is moved to philosophical levels through the use of questions as in this excerpt of discussion of the story 'The Monkey and her Baby' (p 22) with six to seven year olds:

Teacher	Why did the mother think that her baby was best?
Child	Because it was beautiful. She thought it was beautiful.
Child	She thought it was beautiful because she was the mother.
Teacher	What does it mean to be beautiful?
Child	It means someone thinks you are lovely.
Child	You are perfect …
Child	Good to look at.
Teacher	Can you be beautiful even if no-one thinks you are lovely?
Child	No. You can't be beautiful if no-one thinks you are beautiful.
Child	You can be beautiful inside, you can *feel* beautiful …

Philosophy for Children follows the approach of Socrates in using questions as the stimulus to enquiry. The Socratic teacher is not in the traditional role of authority imparting knowledge and telling children what to think and believe. The teacher is Socratic in the sense of being a guide who understands how to question, enquire and explore issues in a way that help others, namely their children, to do the same. The approach is an adventure in ideas as both teacher and learner explore issues together.

Research in over thirty countries around the world show that children can take great strides in their conceptual understanding, in their ability to interrogate the world and in the growth of their self confidence as thinkers and learners through Philosophy for Children. They learn the habits of intelligent thinking, including how to:

- ask questions and raise topics for discussion
- develop their own ideas, views and theories
- give reasons for what they think
- explain and argue their point of view with others
- listen to and consider the views of others
- change their ideas in the light of good reasons and evidence.

Even four year olds can benefit from the process of community of enquiry. They often find it easier to make statements about the story, like 'The king was wicked', than to ask questions. These can be recorded on the board (with the child's name) and become a focus for discussion, for example by asking: 'What do you mean by that?' or by focusing on a key word such as: 'What does 'wicked' mean?' Even if they are not capable of entering into philosophical discussion, it introduces them to the experience and to the habits of mind that prepare them for higher order thinking in the future. As one nursery teacher said: 'My Stories for Thinking lessons are pre-philosophical. I am preparing my children for the kinds of thinking and reasoning I hope my children will grow into. After all they are the thinkers of the future, and it is never too early to start them on it.'

Often young children will choose to call philosophical discussion by its proper name – Philosophy, if they are introduced to the term. The lesson may have different names, such as Stories for Thinking, Thinking Circle or even Literacy Hour. Whatever it is called, children are often quick to see the value of having time set aside to think through stories. Kirandeep, aged eight, says philosophy discussions are important because 'thinking is what we are here for.' Karen, aged eight, says she likes Stories for Thinking lessons because they makes stories 'a kind of puzzle.' I hope you and your children will also find these stories puzzling and enjoyable.

Further reading

Cam P (1995), *Thinking Together*, Sydney: Hale & Iremonger

de Haan C, MacColl S & McCutcheon L (1995), *Philosophy With Kids*, Melbourne: Longman

Fisher, R (1995), *Teaching Children to Think*, Cheltenham: Stanley Thornes

Fisher R (1995), *Teaching Children to Learn,* Cheltenham: Stanley Thornes

Fisher R (1996), *Stories for Thinking*, Oxford: Nash Pollock Publishing

Fisher R (1997), *Poems for Thinking*, Oxford: Nash Pollock Publishing

Fisher R (1997), *Games for Thinking*, Oxford: Nash Pollock Publishing

Fisher R (1998), *Teaching Thinking: Philosophical Enquiry in the Classroom*, London: Cassell

Fisher R (1999), *Head Start: How to Develop Your Child's Mind,* London: Souvenir Press

Matthews, GB (1980), *Philosophy and the Young Child,* London: Harvard University Press

Murris K (1992), *Teaching Philosophy with Picture Books,* London: Infonet Publications

Sprod T (1993), *Books into Ideas,* Cheltenham, Victoria (Aus.): Hawker Brownlow Education

Further Information

SAPERE (Society for the Advancement of Philosophical Enquiry and Reflection in Education)
Website: www.sapere.net

ROBERT FISHER
Dr Robert Fisher, Brunel University, 300 St. Margarets Road, Twickenham TW1 1PT
Website: www.teachingthinking.net

Stories and Themes

1 Foolish Dan

There was once a boy called Dan who lived with his mother in a hut in the woods. They were a poor family and one day there was no food to eat in the house. Dan's mother said, 'All we have left is a bag of seeds. Take them to market and sell them. Then with the money you can buy some food for us to eat.'

So Dan took the bag of seeds and set off for market, but soon he forgot all that his mother had said. It was a hot day. 'I wish I had a hat,' said Dan, 'to shade my head.' Just then a man came along the road. He had a big hat on his head.

'Good day,' said Dan. 'I wonder if you would let me have your hat for these seeds.' The man agreed, for the seeds were worth more than his old hat.

Dan went off with the hat on his head. He forgot all about going to market to buy food for his mother. After a while he began to feel thirsty, so he sat under a tree and fanned himself with his hat. Soon an old woman came by with a jug of water.

'Good day,' said Dan. 'Would you give me that jug of water for this hat?' The old woman liked the look of the hat, so she gave Dan the jug of water, and went on her way with his hat.

Dan drank all the water and walked on with the empty jug in his hand. He had forgotten all about the market and what he had been sent to do. Soon he began to feel hungry. How could he find something to eat? Just then he saw a boy coming towards him eating an apple.

'Good day,' said Dan. 'May I have the rest of your apple for this jug? I am very hungry.' The boy saw the jug had some value, so he gave Dan his apple, and went off with the jug.

Dan ate the apple, but still felt hungry. 'I think I'll go home now,' he thought. 'Mother is sure to find me something to eat.'

When he got home his mother said, 'Have you sold the seeds? What food have you brought home from market?'

'Oh dear,' said Dan. 'I forgot!'

'You forgot? You forgot? I'll teach you not to forget,' said his mother. She picked up the rolling pin and chased him from the house.

That night Dan went to bed a very hungry boy.

(English folktale)

Thinking about the story

Key question: What does the story mean?

1 Who was Dan?

2 What did Dan's mother ask him to do? Why?

3 What did Dan forget? Why did he forget?

4 What was the first thing Dan wanted on the way to the market? Why did he want it?

5 Why did the man think the seeds were worth more than the hat?

6 What did Dan exchange the hat for? Why did he do this?

7 What did he exchange the jug for? Why?

8 What happened when Dan went home?

9 What would you have said to Dan if you were his mother?

10 What should Dan or his mother do next?

Thinking about forgetting

Key question: What helps you to remember ?

1 Do you find it easy to remember things? Give an example.

2 Is it possible to remember everything?

3 What are the most important things to remember?

4 What things are not worth remembering?

5 What helps you to remember?

6 Is it easier to remember something you have heard or something you have seen?

7 Why do you forget things?

8 Can you remember something that never happened?

9 Is it possible to lose your memory and forget everything?

10 What is the best thing you can remember? Why is it good to remember?

Further activities

- Ask the children to sequence the events in the story, using sentences or pictures.

- Read sentences in the story, missing out a word. Can children guess the missing word(s)?

- Identify the nouns in the story. Can children put them in alphabetical order?

- Play memory games e.g. 'Kim's Game'. One person chooses seven objects to put on a tray. The other players look at the objects. The objects are then covered by a cloth. Players try to name or draw the objects. How many can they remember?

- 'Suitcase'. Pretend you are packing a bag to go on holiday. One person begins: 'I packed my bag and I put in a ...' (naming an item). The next player repeats the whole sentence, and adds another item. Take turns repeating the list and adding an item. How many different items can you remember?

- Make a list of important things (or rules) to remember. Vote on their order of importance.

2 Lazy Jack

Jack was a lazy boy. He lived with his mother in a tiny cottage. They were very poor. Jack had no father, and his mother worked very hard every day, spinning wool. But Jack never lifted a finger to help her. He just sat around all day or stayed snoozing in his bed. No wonder they called him Lazy Jack.

One day his mother said to him, 'If you don't find a job by tomorrow I'll throw you out of the house. Off you go, and don't come back till you find one.'

Lazy Jack went to the local farmer who gave him a job for a day. That evening the farmer gave Jack a £10 note for his work. On the way home Jack took the note out to look at it, but just then a gust of wind blew the note out of his hand and he lost it.

His mother was very angry. 'You should have put it in your pocket,' she said.

'I'll do it next time,' said Lazy Jack.

The next day Jack helped in a dairy, and he was given a jug of milk to take home with him. Remembering what his mother said he poured the milk into his pocket. When he got home his mother was even more angry. ' You should have carried it on our head!' she shouted.

'I'll do that next time,' said Lazy Jack.

Next day Jack got a job with another farmer, and was given a large packet of butter for helping him. Jack set off home with the butter carefully balanced on his head. It was very sunny that day and the butter began to melt. Gradually it ran down his hair and neck until he was covered in it. 'You silly boy!' screamed his mother. 'You should have carried it under your coat!'

'I'll do it next time,' said Lazy Jack.

Next day Jack worked for a farmer who gave him a donkey for helping. Jack picked the animal up and tried to put it under his coat. Holding onto the struggling donkey Jack headed for home.

On his way home Jack passed the house of a sad girl who had never laughed in her life. No one could even make her smile. But when she saw Jack trying to hold a donkey under his jacket she rubbed her eyes in amazement. First she smiled, then she began to laugh.

Jack fell in love with the laughing girl and they soon got married. Jack promised her that from that day he would now work hard and stop his lazy ways. And he said they would never call him Lazy Jack again.

(European folktale)

Thinking about the story

Key question: What does the story mean?

1   Why did they call him Lazy Jack?
2   What did Jack do all day? What work did his mother do?
3   What did his mother say to him?
4   What was the first job that Jack did?
5   What happened to the money the farmer gave him?
6   What should Jack have done with the money?
7   What other jobs did Jack get?
8   When Jack kept saying 'I'll do it next time?' what happened?
9   How did he make the girl laugh? Why did she laugh?
10 Do you think Lazy Jack changed his ways? Why, or why not?

Thinking about being lazy

Key question: What is it to be lazy?

1   Are you ever lazy? Give an example of being lazy.
2   What does 'being lazy' mean?
3   What is the opposite of being lazy?
4   Can you work hard all the time? Why, or why not?
5   Do you know anyone who is lazy? Give an example.
6   What is the hardest work you have to do? What helps you to do it?
7   Should children help their mothers or fathers at home? What should they do?
8   Should children get something for helping at home? Why or why not?
9   Is it good to be lazy? Why or why not?
10 Who works hardest at school, children or teachers?

Further activities

- Children retell the story sitting in a circle, teacher claps hands to move narration to next child.

- Show a copy of the story with some of the words missing (or covered up). Can they guess what the missing words are to make sense of the story?

- Identify the ten hardest (longest) words in the story. Write them on flashcards and see if the children can recognise the words/match them to pictures.

- Draw a scene from the story for others to guess. Write a description on the back.

- Think of ways of carrying/transporting things; find illustrations in information books.

3 The Pretend Doctor

There was once a man who earned his living by mending shoes. He was a lazy man, and never finished a job properly. The shoes he repaired always fell apart. People got to know that his work was bad, and stopped bringing their shoes for him to mend. So the man decided to move to a new town. There he could pretend to be whoever he liked and nobody would know. He decided he would make some easy money by pretending to be a doctor.

When he arrived in the town, he put up notices saying that he was a great doctor and could cure people of anything, for a price.

His first visitor was a woman who told him that her friend was suffering from bad eyes. 'Ah,' said the pretend doctor, 'I'm very good at eyes. I'll cure her in no time with my special oil.'

So the pretend doctor went to the woman's house, and took out of his bag a jar of cooking oil. 'Close your eyes,' he said, 'while I rub the oil in.' She closed her eyes while he rubbed the oil on. 'Good,' he said, 'now keep them closed while the medicine does its work.'

The woman sat there with her eyes shut while the pretend doctor put into his bag whatever he could find that was valuable from the old woman's house. When his bag was full, he said to the woman, 'Now you can open your eyes. I'm sure you feel much better. That will be ten pounds, please.'

The old woman rubbed her eyes. They felt as bad as ever. 'I'm not going to pay you,' she said. 'My eyes are as bad as ever.'

'Oh well,' said the man, 'cures always take time to work. You can have the rest of the oil for only five pounds.'

'Five pounds!' exclaimed the woman.

'Well, you see, it is a very special oil,' said the pretend doctor.

'No, I don't see,' said the woman, 'that's the trouble. I'm going to tell the King about you.'

The man quickly picked up his bag and left.

The old woman went to see the King and complained, 'Before, I could see everything in my house, and now I can't see many of my things.' The King sent for the pretend doctor.

The man came, and when he saw the King he said, 'Oh dear, you do look ill. I've got something that will cure you in no time.'

'Can you cure someone who has been poisoned?' asked the king.

'Certainly, Your Majesty, I have a cure right here.' The man took out a bag of powder.

'Good,' said the King. 'Here is some deadly poison.' He took out a small bottle, and poured it into a glass. 'Now you drink this,' said the King, 'and show me if your cure works. If it does I will pay you well.'

The man took the glass of poison. He began to tremble. His hand started to shake. He wasn't feeling very well. He looked at the poison. There was nothing for it. He had to confess that he couldn't cure poison and that he wasn't a proper doctor.

The old woman got all her things back, and the pretend doctor was sent to jail. Never again would he pretend to be something that he wasn't.

(European folktale)

Thinking about the story

Key question: What does the story mean?

1   What job did the man do before he pretended to be a doctor?
2   Why did people not take their shoes to him?
3   What did the man decide to do to make some money?
4   Did the man tell lies? What lies did the man tell?
5   How did he pretend to cure the old woman?
6   Why did the old woman not pay for the oil?
7   What did the King ask the doctor to do?
8   What did the pretend doctor confess? What does it mean, to 'confess'?
9   Why was the man sent to jail? What had he done wrong?
10   Do you think the man had learnt a lesson?

Thinking about pretending

Key question: What does pretending mean ?

1   What is a *pretend* doctor?
2   Have you ever pretended to be someone you weren't ?
3   When you pretend to be someone else, what do you do?
4   When you pretend to be someone else, do you believe you *are* that person?
5   When you pretend, do you try to fool yourself, or fool others, or both?
6   Do you know anyone who pretends to be what they are not?
7   Is pretending the same as lying?
8   Why do some people pretend to be who they are not?
9   Are some people always pretending? Do some people never pretend?
10   When is it right to pretend? When is it wrong to pretend?

Further activities

*   Tell the story from the old woman's point of view.
*   Find some speech marks in the story. Rewrite some dialogue in speech bubbles linked to a picture of a character.
*   Cover a word in the text. Can the children predict what the missing word is?
*   Create a cartoon version of the story; draw and label a picture for each scene.
*   Make up an advertisement for something that will cure an illness or a problem.

4 The Monkey and her Baby

One day the king of the gods decided to find out which of the animals had the most beautiful baby. So he asked every kind of animal to come and show him their baby. He said he would give the animal with the most beautiful baby a big prize.

All the animals said they would come, for they all wanted to win the prize for having the most beautiful baby.

The animals came in a long line, each with a baby to show the king. There was a cow and her calf, a dog and her puppy, a cat and her kitten, a sheep with her little lamb, a lion and her cub, a goat and her kid – in fact all the animals you can think of, with their babies.

They all passed in front of the king. He looked carefully at each baby to see which was the most beautiful. All the animals wondered which baby the king would choose to win the prize.

Having seen all the animals in the big parade, the king of the gods was just about to say who the winner was when a monkey came running in carrying her baby. She thrust her baby into the king's arms.

The king stared down at the little creature with its wrinkled face and screwed-up eyes. 'Whatever is this?' asked the king.

The king thought it was the ugliest thing he had ever seen. He held the baby well away from himself and stared at it.

'Take it away!' he said. 'It is the ugliest baby I have ever seen!'

All the other animals began to laugh.

The mother monkey took her baby and cuddled it in her arms. 'I don't care what you say,' she said. 'You can give the prize to whoever you like. I know that my baby is the most beautiful baby of all!'

Monkeys, like all mothers, think that their own child is the best.

(African folktale)

Thinking about the story

Key question: What does the story mean?

1   Why did the animals come to see the king of the gods?
2   What animals came to see the king?
3   Which is your favourite baby animal? Why is it your favourite?
4   Which animal was the last to come in?
5   What did the king think of the baby monkey?
6   Why did he think this? Do you agree?
7   What did the mother monkey think of her baby?
8   Why did she think this?
9   Do you think all mothers think their babies are the best? Why is this?
10 Do you think babies are beautiful? Can you say why?

Thinking about beauty

Key question: What is beautiful?

1   What do we mean when we say something is beautiful?
2   Can you think of something that is beautiful to look at?
3   What (or what else) is beautiful to look at? Why is it beautiful?
4   Does everyone agree about what things are beautiful? Why?
5   Can things you hear be beautiful? Can you give an example?
6   Can a smell be beautiful? What smells are beautiful?
7   Can something be a beautiful taste? What do you think tastes beautiful?
8   Can something be beautiful to touch? What is beautiful to touch?
9   Do you ever have a beautiful feeling?
10 What is a beautiful person? Do you know someone who is beautiful?

Further activities

- Discuss similarities and differences between baby/adult animals, or between babies/children/adults.
- Write 'I love to see/hear/taste/touch ...'. Children complete sentences in their own words.
- Match the words for animals (or baby animals) with their pictures.
- Display objects or pictures you think are beautiful. Describe, draw or paint one of these.
- Make a survey of children's ideas of the most beautiful sight/smell/taste, and draw a graph of the results.

5 The Brave Mice

One day there were some mice who were afraid of nothing, except for the old cat who kept chasing them. She was a clever cat. She could move softly, without a sound, and when she pounced she was as fast as lightning and had deadly sharp claws.

One day the mice decided that they must do something about the cat. So they called a meeting of all the mice to talk about the problem. What could they do to stop the cat chasing and catching them?

The mice put forward many plans to stop the cat. One mouse said, 'Perhaps we should take turns to follow the cat so we would always know where the cat was?'

'No,' said the other mice, 'that is too dangerous.'

Another mouse said, 'Perhaps we should make a trap for the cat to fall into?'

'No,' said the other mice, 'that is too difficult.'

Another mouse said, ' Perhaps we should take food to the cat and try to be friends?'

'No,' said the other mice, 'that would never work.'

The meeting went on far into the night, but none of the plans they thought of seemed to be any good.

'I have an idea,' said an old grey mouse, who was thought to be very wise. 'I know how we can all keep out of the cat's way. Let us hang a bell around the cat's neck. Then, every time she moves we will hear it ring. We shall hear her coming, and be able to run way.'

The mice thought this was a very good idea. 'Good idea! Good idea!' they squeaked and one of them ran off to get a bell.

'Now,' said the old mouse, 'there's only one more thing to decide.'

'What is that?' asked the other mice.

'Now which one of you is going to hang the bell around the cat's neck?' asked the old grey mouse.

This time there was silence.

Then all the mice spoke at once. 'Not I! Not I! Not I!' said the mice, and they all ran back into their holes.

(Aesop's fable)

Thinking about the story

Key question: What does the story mean?

1 Why did the mice want to get rid of the cat?
2 Why do cats chase mice? Do they chase anything else?
3 In what ways was the cat clever?
4 Did the mice like being chased by the cat? Why?
5 Why did the mice meet together?
6 What plans did they think of to stop the cat?
7 What is a plan?
8 What plan could you think of to stop the cat?
9 Can you think of a way the mice could get a bell around the cat's neck?
10 Were they brave mice? What other title would you give the story?

Thinking about being brave

Key question: What does being brave mean ?

1 Can you describe someone who is brave?
2 Have you ever been brave? Can you say when?
3 Can you think of someone who has been brave? How were they brave?
4 What people have jobs where they have to be brave?
5 What is the opposite of being brave?
6 Is everyone brave, or are some people more brave than others? Give an example.
7 Are people frightened of some things? Why?
8 Can you be scared and brave at the same time?
9 If you are feeling scared, what can you do to help you feel more brave?
10 When are you scared? Why are you scared? Is it good to be scared?

Further activities

• Retell the story, pretending you are one of the mice.
• Finish the sentence 'One day a mouse ...' in as many ways as you can.
• Think of as many words as you can, and their opposites, to describe a cat or mouse e.g. .clever cat/silly cat, brave cat/scared cat etc.
• Find out all you can about the lives of mice, or cats.
• Discuss and draw your own plan to show how the mice could stop the cat chasing them. (See also the probability game 'Cat and Mouse' in *Games for Thinking* p 107)

6 The Jar of Ants

One evening a man hurried home to his wife with some exciting news. He said, 'Someone told me today that on the hill there is a large tree, and under that tree many years ago a jar of gold was buried. The person who buried the gold has died, and it is there waiting to be dug up. I wonder if it could be true?'

There is only one way to find out,' said his wife.

'Let's go to bed early tonight and dig it up first thing tomorrow morning,' said the man.

Next door there lived a nosy neighbour who loved to know everybody's business. That evening he had pressed his ear close to the wall. He had heard every word that the man and his wife had said. As he listened he smiled at the thought of the gold. At once he rushed off, with his spade in his hand, to dig up the jar before the man and his wife could.

When he reached the hill he saw one large tree, and began to dig, and thought, 'Will I find the jar? Will I find the gold? Will I be rich for evermore?'

He dug and dug, but found nothing but earth and stones. Then... clink! His spade hit a heavy object. What was it? He dug deeper and found a large jar. He lifted the jar out of the earth and reached inside for the gold. But to his horror he found not gold, but hundreds of ants!

The man was very angry. He covered the jar and ran back to the house of the husband and wife. He climbed with the jar onto the roof of their house and loosened a tile. Through the gap he could see the bed on which the man and wife lay sleeping. Now he would get his revenge!

He held the jar ready and shouted, 'You lied to me, so here are some ants for you to eat!'

Then he emptied the jar through the hole down onto where the man and wife slept. But all he could hear was the sound of falling coins.

The husband awoke. 'Amazing!' he said. 'Gold is raining down from heaven.' The man and wife stared at their bed. It was covered in gold coins.

Up on the roof the man stared into the jar – it was empty.

(Chinese folktale)

Thinking about the story

Key question: What does the story mean?

1   How did the man hear about the jar of gold?
2   Why did the man think the story was true? Could it have been true?
3   How could the man next door hear what the man and wife were saying?
4   What sort of person was he? Why did he want to hear what they were saying?
5   Is it right to listen in secret to what others are saying? Why?
6   What was in the jar that the man dug up? How do you know?
7   Why did he climb on the roof with the jar? What was his plan?
8   Did his plan work? Why?
9   What do you think happens after the story ends?
10 Could the story have really happened? Why or why not?

Thinking about real and not real

Key question: What is real?

1   Some things are real, some are not real. What can you see that is real?
2   Can you think of something which is not real? Why is it not real?
3   What is a fairy tale? Could a fairy tale really happen?
4   Can you think of a story that could really happen?
5   Can you think of a story that could never really happen?
6   Are the characters you see in a film or on TV real?
7   We call some stories fiction. What is fiction? Give an example.
8   Some stories are non-fiction. What is non-fiction? Give an example.
9   Can people think things are real which are not real? Give an example.
10 How do you find out if something is really true?

Further activities

*   Retell the story in mime. Show how to make detailed actions in mime e.g. unscrewing a jar lid.
*   Discuss why gold is precious, and what things are coloured gold. Write sentences beginning 'Gold is...'
*   Play Hunt the Vowel. How many words can you find beginning with a, e, i, o, u?
*   Look at pictures of ants and other insects; discuss similarities and differences.
*   Draw imaginary insects.

7 The Miller, his Son and the Donkey

One hot day a miller and his son were taking their donkey to market so that they could sell it. They had not gone far along the road when they met some girls.

'How silly you are,' said one of the girls, 'walking with a donkey. Why don't you ride the donkey?'

So the miller sat his son on the donkey, and off they went, clip-clop-clip-clop, towards the town, the miller walking and his son riding.

After a while they met two old men. One old man said to the other, 'Look at that lazy boy riding while his poor father walks. Young people are so selfish!'

Hearing this the miller's son jumped down from the donkey, and helped his father up on to the donkey's back. And off they went, clip-clop, towards the town, the miller riding on the donkey.

On their way they passed some women working in the fields. 'You cruel man,' said one of the women. 'Fancy riding on the donkey while your poor son has to walk. Shame on you!'

So the miller, who was a kind man, picked up his son and placed the boy behind him on the donkey's back. And they both rode on the donkey.

As they drew near to the town they were stopped by a shepherd, who said, 'That is no way to treat a donkey! Two of you on his back is much too heavy for the poor animal. You are better able to carry the donkey than he is to carry you.' So they did as the shepherd said.

The miller and his son climbed down from the donkey's back. They tied the donkey's legs to a pole. They lifted the pole up and carried it with the donkey upside down between them. And they staggered off towards the market.

As they were crossing a bridge, people began to point and laugh at the strange sight of a donkey being carried on a pole by the man and the boy. The noise of their laughing so frightened the poor donkey that he began to kick and struggle. The miller and his son tried to keep hold of him, but the donkey struggled so much that they all fell into the river with a great SPLASH!

They were soon fished out, wet, but none the worse. As they went home, the miller and his son decided that in future they would not just do what other people said, but would think for themselves.

(French folktale)

Thinking about the story

Key question: What does the story mean?

1 Why do you think the miller and his son were going to market?
2 What did the girls say? What did the miller and his son do then?
3 What did the two old men say? What did the miller and his son do then?
4 What did the women working in the fields say? What the miller do then?
5 What did the shepherd say? What did the miller and his son do then?
6 Why did the miller and his son fall into the river? What happened then?
7 How do you think they should have travelled to market with the donkey?
8 Why did they always do what other people said they should do?
9 How do you think they went to market in the future?
10 What is the moral of the story (what lesson had the man and boy learnt)?

Thinking about thinking for yourself

Key question: What is thinking for yourself ?

1 Is it a good thing to do what other people tell you? Give an example.
2 When do you do what other people tell you?
3 Do you always do what other people tell you? When might it be better to think for yourself?
4 Has someone ever told you to do something silly? If so, what was it?
5 Has anyone told you to do something wrong? If so, what happened?
6 Do you ever tell other people what to do? When and why?
7 Do other people sometimes not do what you say? Give an example.
8 Do people ever 'dare' you to do things? When, and why?
9 Do you ever 'dare' other people to do things? When, and why?
10 Can you give an example of when you have thought for yourself?

Further activities

- Ask the children to re-tell the sequence of the story on a map or time line.
- Write 'I went to market and I bought ...' Each child in turn names an item which is added to a list. The list is then covered and children are asked to remember one item from the list.
- Set up a 'market', label items and play buying/selling/bargaining games.
- Draw a scene from the story, and write a description of it.
- Make up a play about someone who did something silly because someone told them to.

8 The Town Mouse and the Country Mouse

Once upon a time the Country Mouse invited his cousin the Town Mouse to stay with him.

The Country Mouse lived alone under a hedge in the corner of a field. The Country Mouse did not have fine food but he was happy to share what he had with the Town Mouse. There were grains of wheat, nuts and some stale cheese. The Town Mouse did not think much of this country food. He nibbled a bit and then turned up his nose.

'Dear cousin,' he said, 'how can you eat such plain food? Come and visit me in the city. I'll give you a good dinner. Besides, life in the country is so dull. Nothing ever seems to happen. There is always a lot going on in the town, and food is just left lying around for you to eat.'

So the Country Mouse agreed to go back with the Town Mouse to the big city where he lived. By the time they arrived at the Town Mouse's home it was dark. They went in through a hole in the wall. The Town Mouse led the Country Mouse right into a large dining room. On the table they saw what was left of a fine dinner, with food of every kind.

'Is this food all for us?' asked the Country Mouse.

'Of course. Didn't I tell you?' said the Town Mouse. 'Help yourself.'

So the two mice climbed onto the table and were soon eating jam and cake, cheese and trifle and many other tasty foods. Then something frightening happened.

'Listen! What is that?' said the Country Mouse. There was hardly a sound but they could see something creeping towards them. What was it?

'It's a cat! Run for your life!' cried the Town Mouse.

The cat leapt at them with sharp claws. The mice jumped from the table, and ran for their lives. The cat chased them but they just managed to reach their hole in time.

When the Country Mouse got his breath back he had made up his mind what to say to the Town Mouse. The Country Mouse thanked the Town Mouse for inviting him, but said he would go back to the country.

'Why?' asked the Town Mouse.

'I would rather eat my simple food in peace than risk being caught by the cat,' said the Country Mouse. And he ran back as fast as his legs would carry him to his safe country life.

(Aesop's fable)

Thinking about the story

Key question: What does the story mean?

1   The Town Mouse was the Country Mouse's cousin. What is a cousin?
2   Where did the Country Mouse live? Why did he live there?
3   What food did the Country Mouse eat? Where did he get it from?
4   What did the Town Mouse think of the country? Why did he think that?
5   Where did the Town Mouse live? Why did he live there?
6   What food did the Town Mouse eat? Where did he get it from?
7   What frightened the Country Mouse? Why was he frightened?
8   Why did the cat chase the mice?
9   Why did the Country Mouse want to go home?
10 Which would you rather be, a Country Mouse or Town Mouse? Why?

Thinking about differences

Key question: Why are people different ?

1   Is everybody different?
2   Are people different in the way they look, feel or think?
3   Can any two people be exactly the same?
4   In what ways are other people the same as you?
5   In what ways are you different from other people?
6   Is it good to be different from other people? Why, or why not?
7   Would it be good if everyone was the same? Why, or why not?
8   Are you the same as you were last year, or different?
9   Will you be the same next year as you are now, or different?
10 What would you like to change about yourself?

Further activities

*   Ask children to write or tell the story from the point of view of the Country or Town Mouse.

*   Identify and discuss the use of full stops, exclamation and question marks in the story.

*   List words that describe mice, and discuss the meanings of these words.

*   Discuss the differences in children's lives from other children e.g in the past, from other parts of the country, or from other countries.

*   Find and read more Aesop's fables and discuss what the moral of each story is.

9 The Wise Man of Ireland and his Cake

Once upon a time the Wise Man of Ireland was on his travels. It was morning, the birds were singing and the sun was shining. The Wise Man of Ireland was happy, but for one thing. He was hungry. He had not had anything to eat all day.

The Wise Man sat on a rock by the road and felt his tummy rumble with hunger. Then he remembered he had a cake in his pocket. He took it out and unwrapped it, licking his lips. The cake looked delicious.

Just as he was about to take a large bite he saw a band of people coming towards him along the road. They were all carrying shopping bags and looked very tired. The Wise Man of Ireland felt sorry for them, so he held out his piece of cake. 'Would you like to share my cake?' he asked.

The group of people were a man and his six children, three sons and three daughters. They stopped, looked at the cake and nodded. So the Wise Man divided his cake into eight pieces, and handed seven of them over to the family. There was only enough for a small piece each.

'I am sorry it is so little,' said the Wise Man.

'Oh, a gift is never little,' replied the man, as he took a piece of the Wise Man's cake.

The children also took a piece each, and ate it. The Wise Man only had a small bit left for himself, and soon it was gone.

When they had all finished the bearded man said, 'Now we have eaten your cake, what shall we do with the food that we have brought with us? My wife packed it for our trip to market.' Sure enough each one had with them a packet of food in their shopping bags. They didn't feel hungry now after eating the Wise Man's cake.

'It would be a pity to waste our food,' said the man. 'Perhaps you would share it with us,' he said to the Wise Man. The Wise Man was still feeling very hungry and was pleased to agree.

So each one of them divided their packet of food into half, and handed it over to the Wise Man. The Wise Man was amazed to see how much food he was getting. The six children and the bearded man waved goodbye to the Wise Man and continued on their way. 'What did I do,' he wondered, 'to get all this lovely food?'

(Irish folktale)

Thinking about the story

Key question: What does the story mean?

1   Why was the Wise Man hungry?
2   How did he know he was hungry?
3   What did he find to eat?
4   Who did he share his cake with?
5   How many pieces of cake did he give to the family?
6   Where was the family going?
7   What did the family have with them?
8   Why did the family share their food with the Wise Man?
9   How did the Wise Man end up having so much food?
10   What sort of person was the Wise Man of Ireland?

Thinking about sharing

Key question: What is a fair share?

1   Do you ever share things with other people? Give an example.
2   Do other people share things with you? Give an example.
3   What do you share at home?
4   What do you share at school?
5   What things don't you share?
6   Is it a good thing to share with others? Why or why not?
7   Has there ever been a time when others have not shared things with you?
8   Has there ever been a time when you have not shared things with other people?
9   Should people who have food share it with people who are hungry?
10   Sometimes people talk of having a 'fair share' of something. What is a fair share?

Further activities

- Discuss and write about the things the children would take with them on a journey.
- Ask the children to listen as you read a sentence. Make a deliberate mistake. Can they spot the mistake(s) you make?
- Hunt for words from the story beginning with a letter or sound of your or their choice.
- Show how to divide a cake (or picture of a cake) into eight pieces.
- Discuss, write the recipe and make a cake for a special occasion to share with other people.

10 The Three Wishes

There was once an old man. Although he worked hard every day of his life, he was very poor. One day as he was walking home from work he said to himself, 'If only I could have three wishes, then all my troubles would be over.'

Just then a small man dressed in green appeared. 'I am here to help you,' said the elf. 'I will grant you your three wishes. Whatever you wish will be yours. But take care what you do with them.'

The old man could not believe his luck. He ran home to tell his wife, without stopping even to say 'thank you' to the elf.

'Wife! Wife!' he shouted. 'Good news! The little people have granted us three wishes. We can have anything we like.'

'Oh good,' said the wife. 'We can get out of this little old cottage and get ourselves a lovely new house.'

'Oh no,' said the old man. 'We need a new car first.'

'I want a lovely new dress,' said the wife. 'In fact a whole new wardrobe of dresses.'

'Oh no you don't,' said the old man. 'I need clothes more than you do. I shall get myself a new suit – you've got plenty of dresses.'

'Oh no I haven't,' said the wife.

'Oh yes you have,' shouted her husband, and soon they were having a great row.

After a while the old man said, 'Let's stop arguing and have something to eat. We can decide what we really want after supper.'

The wife agreed. The old man sat down at the table, and his wife brought out their evening meal – one sausage each. The old man was hungry. He licked his lips at the sight of the sausage.

'Ooh, I wish this sausage was as big as my arm!' he said.

Wham! The sausage swelled and swelled until it was as long and fat as the old man's arm.

'Now look what you've done,' scolded his wife. 'You've wasted one of your wishes on a sausage!'

'It wasn't my fault,' moaned the old man.

'Oh yes it was!' said the old woman, and again they started to argue. Then the old man lost his temper and snapped, 'Oh, I wish the sausage was on the end of your nose!'

Wham! The long sausage hung on the end of his wife's nose. She burst into tears. She cried and she cried but the sausage stayed stuck on the end of her nose. At last the old man said, 'Oh I wish that sausage would go!'

Wham! The sausage flew from the wife's nose right out of the window. Instead of being pleased the wife was more angry than ever.

'Look, you've used up all our wishes,' she cried.

The old man sat there scratching his head. 'Why did it all go wrong?' he asked.

(English folktale)

Thinking about the story

Key question: What does the story mean?

1   Was the old man rich or poor? How do you know?
2   What did he say as he walked home from work?
3   Who appeared dressed in green? What kind of person was he?
4   What did the elf say to the old man? Why did he say it?
5   What happened when he went home to tell his wife?
6   What did the old man want with his wishes?
7   What did his wife want with her wishes?
8   What did they have for supper? What happened next?
9   Why did it go all wrong?
10 What kind of story is this?

Thinking about wishing

Key question: What is a wish?

1   What does it mean to wish for something?
2   Have you ever wished for something? Did you get it?
3   Some people wish for things, some pray for things. Is wishing the same as praying?
4   Can you help wishes come true? How?
5   Do you ever wish for something for other people?
6   Do you think everyone wishes for something?
7   Does wishing for something help it to happen?
8   Are there ever times when you are asked to make a wish?
9   If you had one wish for yourself, what would it be?
10 If you had one wish for others (or the world), what would it be?

Further activities

- Make a story ladder, writing a key incident on each rung (see p 76).
- Make a Book of Wishes, each writing a wish for themselves and a wish for others.
- Show the text of the story with key words missing. Can children predict the missing words?
- Draw a picture of someone wishing (draw or write the wish in a thought-bubble).
- Interview people. Ask them what their wish for themselves, and the world, would be.

11 The Angry Lion

There was once a cruel lion who enjoyed killing all the animals that came his way, whether he was hungry or not. So the animals met to discuss the problem. If the lion carried on like this there would soon be no animals left in the forest. What could they do?

The rat had an idea. 'Let us offer the lion one animal to eat, a different kind each day, or he will kill us all.'

The animals agreed, and each day a different animal was chosen to feed the lion. At last came the turn of the rabbits, and they chose the oldest of their kind to be eaten by the lion.

He was a wise old rabbit, and took his time, stopping to nibble the grass on his way to be eaten by the lion. As the lion waited he grew more and more angry.

'Where is the rabbit who is supposed to be coming?' he roared. 'If he is not here soon I shall kill all the animals in the forest. How dare they disobey me, the King of the Jungle!'

Just then the rabbit appeared. The lion pounced. 'Got you!' he growled.

'Take pity on me, great king,' said the rabbit. 'I would have been here before, but on the way I met another lion who told me *he* was the King of the Jungle. I only just managed to escape.'

'What!' roared the lion. 'Is there another lion who pretends to be king? Take me to him. I will eat you later.' The rabbit led the lion to the edge of a large well.

'He's down there,' said the rabbit, 'resting in the cool water after his dinner. Look carefully and you will see him.'

The lion looked down and there in the water he saw a face just like his own. The lion roared and a roar came echoing back. The lion swelled with anger and roared again. The well trembled with its noise.

'How dare you challenge me!' roared the lion. 'I'll show you!' And still snarling with rage the lion leapt into the well. Splash! Down he sank in the deep water and was never seen again.

The rabbit looked into the well, and smiled at his face reflected in the water. Then he ran back to tell the good news to the other animals. The angry lion had gone, and they were free at last.

(Aesop's fable)

Thinking about the story

Key question: What does the story mean?

1 The story says the lion was cruel. What does 'cruel' mean?
2 What did the lion enjoy doing?
3 What problem did the animals have?
4 What was the rat's plan to solve the problem?
5 The story says the rabbit was wise. What does 'wise' mean?
6 What reason did the rabbit give to the lion for being late?
7 Why did the lion think *he* was King of the Jungle?
8 How did the rabbit trick the lion?
9 Why did the lion jump into the well?
10 What kind of story is this? Could it be true? Why?

Thinking about anger

Key question: What does it mean to be angry ?

1 Do you know anyone who gets angry? Who?
2 Why do people get angry?
3 When is it right to feel angry? When is it wrong to feel angry?
4 How can you tell if someone is feeling angry?
5 Can you always tell if someone is feeling angry? Why, or why not?
6 What makes you angry?
7 Can you remember the angriest you have ever been?
8 Can you pretend to be angry? Show me.
9 Is it ever good to feel angry? Why?
10 If you feel angry what should you do?

Further activities

• Ask the children to recall the details of the story in sequence.
• Finish this sentence. 'I get angry when ...'
• Brainstorm all the words connected to the idea of being cruel.
• Act out a play about a parent being angry with a child.
• Draw or paint an 'angry' picture.

12 How Frog Lost his Tail

Once in Africa there lived a frog.

Frog sat in his muddy home at the edge of the pond and felt sad. He thought he was ugly, with a mouth like a large cave, eyes that stuck out like door knobs and a slimy green body. But what made the frog saddest of all was that he had no tail.

All the other animals had a tail - except him.

Each evening Frog watched the forest animals come down to the pond to drink. Frog looked at their long swishy tails and felt sad. So he went to the Sky God and said, 'I am so ugly. Please give me a tail.'

'Very well,' said the Sky God in a voice like thunder. 'I will give you a tail if you will watch my special well and see that it never dries up. The water there is for all to share.' Frog agreed to watch over the Sky God's well, and so the Sky God gave him a lovely new tail.

Frog made himself a new home beside the Sky God's well and spent the time hopping around, showing off his fine new tail. Frog now thought he was the most beautiful creature in the whole world. Having such a large tail made him feel very proud of himself. 'I have the most beautiful tail in the world,' he said.

For a long time it did not rain and all the ponds and wells dried up, except for the special well which was guarded by Frog. When the animals crawled weakly towards him in search of water, Frog would say, 'Who is coming to *my* special well?' The animals would say their names and ask him for water. Then Frog would shout: 'Go away! Go away! There is no water here for you. The well is dry.'

The animals went to the Sky God and told him what the frog had said. So the Sky God thought he would go himself to see what was happening. As he came close to the well Frog shouted, 'Go away! Go away! There's no water here. The well is dry.' The Sky God shook with anger, and decided to punish the Frog. So he took away his lovely long tail and sent him back home to his pond.

Each year the Sky God reminds Frog of the time he was mean to the other animals. In spring when the frog is born as a tadpole he has a long, beautiful tail. But as he grows, his tail shrinks and shrinks until it finally disappears.

The Sky God takes the tail away because Frog was once so selfish.

(African folktale)

Thinking about the story

Key question: What does the story mean?

1   Where did Frog live?
2   Why was Frog feeling sad at the beginning of the story?
3   Why did Frog think he was ugly? Do you think he was ugly?
4   Why did Frog want a tail?
5   Why did the Sky God give him a tail?
6   What is a Sky God?
7   What job did Frog do for the Sky God?
8   Why did other animals come to the Sky God's well?
9   What did Frog say to other animals who came to the well?
10 What did the Sky God take away from Frog? Do you think that was fair? Why?

Thinking about being selfish

Key question: What is being selfish ?

1   The story says Frog was selfish. What does 'being selfish' mean?
2   Why are people selfish?
3   What do people do (or say) when they are feeling selfish?
4   Have people ever been selfish to you? Can you say when?
5   Have you ever been selfish? Can you give an example?
6   Is it always wrong to be selfish?
7   Can you be friends with someone who is selfish?
8   How can you stop someone being selfish?
9   Should you think of other people, or only of yourself? Why?
10 What would the world be like if everyone was selfish all the time?

Further activities

- Ask children to suggest other possible titles for the story. Discuss which is the best title and why.
- Identify speech marks, highlight what characters say, and practise saying their words in different voices. Discuss what 'a voice like thunder' is, and other kinds of voices.
- List the names of all the animals you can think of. Add an alliterative adjective (describing word) to each one e.g. 'fat frog', 'lazy lion'.
- Find examples of other animal fables about how things became.
- Make up your own animal fable about how the frog lost his tai, the leopard got his spots, the tortoise his shell etc.

13 The Four Fools

One day four men went out in a boat on a river. They were going fishing. After a while one of them stood up in the boat. The boat began to rock from side to side. 'What are you standing up for?' asked one of the other men.

'I am looking for fish,' said the man.

A second man stood up and the boat began to rock even more. It is funny how if one person is looking at something everyone else wants to have a look. So the third man stood up. The boat rocked to and fro even more. Then the fourth man stood up. Over went the boat, and the four men fell with a SPLASH into the water.

It was lucky that each man could swim. They all swam to the shore. 'Are we all safe?' asked one of the men.

'I don't know. You had better count us,' said another.

'One, two, three,' counted the first man, pointing to each of the others. But he had forgotten to count himself. 'Oh dear!' he said. 'There are only three. One of us has drowned.'

'Let me count,' said another man. 'One, two, three,' he said, pointing to the others. He also forgot to count himself. 'You are right. One of us has drowned. How sad!' he said. And the four of them began to cry for their lost friend.

Just then a young man came by. 'What is the matter?' he asked.

'Our friend has drowned in the river,' said one of the men. 'There were four of us in the boat and now there are only three. One, two, three!'

'I see,' said the young man. 'Perhaps I can help you. If I can find your friend, would you give me a reward?'

'Oh yes,' said the four fools. 'We will give you our money, if you can find our friend.'

'Well here he is,' said the young man. He tapped the first man on the head. 'One,' he said. Then he hit the second man. 'Two.' He hit the third. 'Three.' And he hit the fourth. 'Four. There is your friend!'

The men were happy because the friend they thought was lost had been found. The young man was happy because he was given a reward. So they were all happy – all five of them.

(Old English folktale)

Thinking about the story

Key question: What does the story mean?

1 How many men went fishing in the boat?

2 Why do you think they were going fishing together?

3 Why did the first man stand up in the boat?

4 Why did the other men stand up in the boat?

5 Why is it dangerous to stand up in a boat?

6 What happened to the four men?

7 Why did they think one of them was missing?

8 What did they think had happened to the missing man?

9 How did the young man help?

10 What is a reward? Do you think the young man deserved a reward?

Thinking about the importance of everyone

Key question: What is important about everyone?

1 Is everyone in our class (group, school, family) important?

2 Why is everyone important?

3 In what ways are we all alike?

4 What is special about human beings?

5 How are we similar to other animals? How are we different from other animals?

6 How are we similar to plants? How are we different?

7 How are you similar to other people? How are you different?

8 Who are the most important people in your life?

9 Who else is important in your life?

10 Is everyone in the world important in some way? Why, or why not?

Further activities

- Read or retell the story, with children adding actions in mime.
- Cover up chosen words in the story. Can children predict the missing word from the rest of the sentence or story?
- Ask children to identify the 'sh' words like 'splash','fish; 'th' words like 'they', 'then, 'other'. Brainstorm other 'sh' and 'th' words.
- Find, learn or make up some counting rhymes e.g. 'One, two , three,/mother caught a flea,/ put it in the teapot/ and made a cup of tea.'
- Discuss important people. Draw concentric circles of important people with the child in the centre.

14 The Forgotten Treasure

Once upon a time there lived a poor shepherd who looked after a small flock of sheep. He lived in a tiny cottage with his wife and family. Every day he walked with his sheep over the hills, helping them to find fresh grass to eat. One day as they were crossing a hill, the shepherd saw a tiny blue flower. He had never seen one quite like it before. Carefully he picked it up and smelt it. Then he tied it to his shepherd's crook and called his sheep to him. He had decided to take this pretty blue flower back with him to give to his wife. She was sure to be pleased. Suddenly a small green man sprang out from behind a tree.

'It's your lucky day!' he said. 'You have found a real treasure. Take that flower and touch the rock on yonder hillside. The rock will open up and all the treasure you find there will be yours. But do not forget the best treasure of all!' And with that the little man disappeared.

The shepherd stood for a moment, wondering what to do. Had he been dreaming? There was only one way to find out. He walked up to the rock with his small blue flower and gently knocked. There was a great rumbling noise and the rock slowly cracked open. The shepherd peeped inside. There were steps in front of him which led down into the darkness. Taking a deep breath the shepherd walked in and went carefully down. At first he could not see anything. Then slowly his eyes got used to the dark. There seemed to be heaps of things on the floor sparkling and winking at him. Gold! Silver! Diamonds!

The shepherd put the tiny blue flower down and, taking the old bag from his shoulder, scooped up as much treasure as he could. As he poured it into his bag a tiny voice whispered in his ear, 'Forget me not! Forget me not!'

But all the shepherd could think of was the gold, the silver and the diamonds. When he had taken as much as he could carry he hurried away back up the stairs, leaving the little blue flower behind. As soon as he was out in the open air … CRASH! The rock closed up again.

He ran home as fast as he could, clutching his bag of treasures. 'Look what I've found!' he shouted as he came in. His family gathered round. 'You've never seen treasure like this,' he panted as he opened the bag.

But inside the bag, there was nothing, nothing but dust and ashes. What had gone wrong? Then he remembered what he had forgotten, the little blue flower.

He raced back to the rock. But it was closed. Try as he might he could find no way in. Then faintly he heard: 'Forget-me-not! Forget-me-not!'

The shepherd then realised he had forgotten the greatest treasure of all.

(Traditional)

Thinking about the story

Key question: What does the story mean?

1   What did the shepherd do each day?
2   What did he find on the hill that he had never seen before?
3   What did he do with the flower?
4   What did the little green man say to him?
5   Who do you think the little green man was?
6   What happened when the rock opened?
7   Why was he so pleased to find the gold, silver and diamonds? .
8   What happened when the shepherd ran home?
9   What had the shepherd forgotten? Why did he forget?
10   What do you think the lesson (moral) of the story is?

Thinking about treasures

Key question: What do you treasure?

1   When you 'treasure' something, what does it mean?
2   Why do some people try to find treasure? What kinds of treasure do they look for?
3   Do you know of anyone who has found any lost treasure?
4   Why do some people hide their treasure so that no-one can find it?
5   If people find treasure, should they be allowed to keep it? Why, or why not?
6   A treasure is something people value very much. What does 'value' mean?
7   Are there things people value (that are very special or important) that are not worth much money?
8   Do you have something that is special or important to you that is not worth much money?
9   Some people say that the most important things are free. What do they mean by this?
10   What do you think the most important thing in your life is?

Further activities

• Ask a child to retell the story as if they were the shepherd and the story happened to them.
• Ask children to put captions to pictures of the story. What are they saying?
• Brainstorm words connected with flowers. Look at pictures/books of plants. Discuss the origin of names like dandelion ('dent du lion'), daisy ('day's eye') and buttercup.
• Draw a picture of an imaginary flower. Name, show and describe the picture.
• Show and discuss pesonal treasures e.g. shells, toys, mementoes.

15 Mercury and the Axe

Long ago in Greece, there was once a man who was cutting wood by a river when his axe slipped from his hand and fell into the water. The river was deep and the current ran fast.

Hard as he looked, the man could see no sign of his axe. It had disappeared forever beneath the swirling waters. Or so he thought. There was nothing he could do. As he sat on the bank, he thought of his lost axe and began to cry.

Mercury, the messenger of the gods, happened to be passing by, and saw the man crying by the riverside. He stopped and asked the man what had happened. When he was told, Mercury felt sorry for the man, so he dived into the fast flowing river. Soon he came up with a golden axe in his hand, and asked the man whether this was the axe he had lost.

'No,' said the woodcutter, 'this is not the axe I lost.'

So Mercury dived down again, and this time came up with a silver axe.

'No,' said the man, 'this is not mine either.'

So the winged god went down for a third time, and came up with the woodcutter's own axe. 'That's the one!' he said, and he thanked Mercury for all the trouble he had taken to find his lost axe. Mercury was so delighted with the honesty of the man that he made him a present of the gold and silver axes as well.

When the woodcutter had finished chopping his wood for the day he went back to his friends who were working in another part of the wood, and told them of his good luck. As they listened, one of the men thought that he too would like to get an axe from Mercury.

So the following day he went down to the river's edge, and threw his axe into the fast flowing waters. When it had disappeared he sat down on the bank and, began to cry as loudly as he could. In a little while Mercury appeared again, and asked the man why he was so sad.

'I've lost my axe,' said the man. 'It just slipped out of my hand as I was cutting wood. It's fallen in the water and I can't find it.'

Mercury felt sorry for the man and once more dived into the cold waters of the river. He soon appeared and shouted to the man, 'I can see something down there. Is your axe a golden one?'

The eyes of the man lit up. 'Oh yes,' he said, 'it is made of real gold.'

The god was angry now, for he knew the man was lying. 'What a shame,' said Mercury, 'the axe that I have found is just an ordinary one. I cannot find your golden axe anywhere in the river. As this is not your axe I'm afraid I cannot help you. I must go and find out who this axe belongs to.' With that Mercury and the axe disappeared.

Left on the bank, without any axe, was a sadder but wiser man.

(Aesop's fable)

Thinking about the story

Key question: What does the story mean?

1 Where was the man cutting wood?

2 Why do you think he was cutting wood?

3 How did the man first lose his axe?

4 Why couldn't he find his axe?

5 How did Mercury help the man? Why did he help him?

6 Who was Mercury? How do you know?

7 Why did Mercury give the man a golden and a silver axe?

8 What trick did the man's friend try to play on Mercury? What happened? Why?

9 The story says the man was left 'sadder but wiser'? What does this mean?

10 What lesson do you think the man learnt? (What is the moral of this story?)

Thinking about telling the truth

Key question: What is truth ?

1 Do you think this is a true story? Why?

2 What do we mean when we say something is true?

3 What do we call something that is not true? What does 'false' mean?

4 What is a lie?

5 What do we call a story which is not true? What is fiction/a fable/a fairy tale?

6 Which man in the story was honest? What does 'honest' mean?

7 Which man in the story was a liar? What does 'liar' mean?

8 Is it better to tell the truth or to tell lies? Why?

9 Have you ever told a lie? Can you say when or why?

10 Is it ever right to tell a lie? Is it ever wrong to tell the truth?

Further activities

- Re-read the story, inviting children to read and act each character's part.

- Ask children to add to phrases from the story to make up complex sentences e.g. 'Long ago in Greece ...', 'The river ...' by adding descriptive words, phrases etc.

- Hunt to find as many words within words as you can e.g. 'wood/cutter' 'for/ever', 'river/side'.

- Sort a list of things or statements, into categories of true and false.

- Make up a story about someone who told a lie and was found out.

16 The Ungrateful Crocodile

One day a holy man was walking along the bed of a dried-up river. It had not rained for weeks and the earth was hard and dry. Suddenly the holy man saw a crocodile lying in the dust panting for breath.

'Please save me,' gasped the crocodile. 'Take me to some water or I shall die.'

The holy man looked at the crocodile and said,'I would like to save you but I've heard that you are fierce and not to be trusted. How do I know you won't eat me once I've rescued you?'

The animal looked hurt. 'Do you really think that I would eat someone who had saved my life?' he asked. 'Is there anyone in the whole world who would do such a cruel thing? Not me, my friend; if you let me live I shall be your friend until my dying day.' A big tear began to roll down the crocodile's face.

The holy man was so sorry for the crocodile that he picked him up, put him into his bag and walked seven miles to the nearest river. Then he let the crocodile out of the bag and told him to crawl into the water.

'Please carry me into the river,' panted the crocodile. 'I am so weak I cannot walk.' The holy man did as he was asked, carried him into the water, and let him go. At once the crocodile seized the holy man's leg and began dragging him under.

'You rogue!' roared the holy man. 'You broke your word.'

'I'm hungry,' said the crocodile and it carried on trying to drown the man.

'Wait!' shouted the holy man. 'There's a jackal, let us ask him whether you are right to eat me or not. If he says that you should, I will stop struggling and you can have me for supper.' The crocodile grumbled but finally agreed to ask the jackal.

When the jackal had heard the story he scratched his head and said, 'I am not very clever. I don't understand how the man brought you to the river. Can you show me?' The crocodile grumbled again and climbed into the holy man's bag.

'Like this,' he growled. The holy man tied up the bag tightly.

'Take him back,' said the jackal, 'and leave him where you found him.'

The holy man laughed as the crocodile writhed in his bag. 'What a clever fellow you are,' he said. 'What a villain *he* is! I saved his life and he tried to take mine. Who would have thought that anyone could be so ungrateful?'

'Nearly everybody!' said the jackal. 'You are too trusting for your own good. Carry on being kind to everyone, but don't expect people to be kind to you in return. It doesn't always work out that way.'

The holy man picked up the bag of crocodile, and realised the jackal was right.

(Story from India)

Thinking about the story

Key question: What does the story mean?

1   What is a 'holy' man? Where was the holy man going?
2   Why did the crocodile think he was going to die?
3   How did the crocodile persuade the holy man to help him?
4   Why did the holy man help him?
5   How did the holy man rescue the crocodile?
6   What happened when they got to the river?
7   Why did the crocodile try to drag the holy man under the water?
8   Why did they speak to the jackal?
9   What was the jackal's advice to the holy man?
10 What do you think the holy man did with the crocodile in the end?

Thinking about kindness

Key question: What is being kind ?

1   The holy man was kind. What does 'being kind' mean?
2   Can you think of someone who is kind? Who?
3   What sorts of things do kind people do? Can you give an example?
4   Is it good to be kind? Why?
5   Have you ever done something kind? Tell us about one kind thing.
6   Is it easy or hard to be kind? Why?
7   Are some people more kind than others? Why ?
8   Can you be kind all the time?
9   Are some people never kind?
10 If you are kind to someone, are they always kind to you?

Further activities

- Ask children to help you create a story map. As they recall the story in sequence, move paper characters around the map.
- Identify speech marks, and rewrite some of the dialogue in speech bubbles next to the pictures of the characters.
- Invite a child to identify a letter and try to find examples of this letter in words in the story at the beginning of words, end and middle.
- Discuss what charity is. Choose a charity, discuss what work it does and ways of raising money for it.
- Write a story about someone being kind to someone who is ungrateful.

17 Midas and the Golden Touch

Many years ago there lived a King named Midas. King Midas was very rich, but he wanted more, and spent all his time trying to get richer.

One day Midas saw an old man being made fun of in his garden. His gardeners had found the old man lying fast asleep, and had tied him up. Midas released the old man, only to find that he was Silenus, servant of the god Dionysus. When Dionysus heard how Midas had freed his old servant, he told the King that he would give him any reward he wished. Midas thought quickly and said, 'I wish that everything I touch would turn to gold!'

'Your wish is granted,' said Dionysus. 'I hope it will make you happy.'

From that moment everything that Midas touched turned to gold. For the next hour or two the King had a wonderful time turning everything that he wished into gold. The flowers and trees in his garden, the statues that stood in the hall, vases and flowers all changed to gold. Midas sat in a chair and smiled, and at once the chair turned to gold. Midas was delighted. Now he would be the richest king in the world.

Midas began to feel hungry, for it was time for lunch. He sat down at his table, which turned to gold at his touch. The plates and dishes too turned to gold. Food was placed on golden dishes, and his wine was poured. He raised the golden glass to his lips but the wine became solid gold. Neither wine nor water could pass his lips. The bread turned gold under his fingers. The meat turned hard and yellow and shiny. There was nothing he could eat. Midas was amazed. What use was his wonderful gift if the food he touched turned to golden metal?

Just then his little daughter came running in from the garden. Of all living things he loved her most. Gently he kissed her hair. At once she turned to gold, and stood still as a statue. All his joy was gone. The world was now a cold and lonely place for Midas.

He left his golden chair and his golden palace, and hurried away to find Dionysus to beg him to take back his terrible gift.

'I will give all my gold,' said Midas, 'for the chance of having my daughter back.'

Dionysus felt sorry for the King, and told him to bathe in a special river. The King did so. When he came out of the water Midas touched the grass. To his joy it stayed green. His golden touch had gone. He bathed his daughter with the water and to his joy she returned to life. They say that you can still find gold at the bottom of the river where Midas bathed. But that would not interest Midas, for he knew that there were things in life more precious than gold.

(Greek legend)

Thinking about the story

Key question: What does the story mean?

1 Who was Midas? When did he live? Where did he live?
2 What happened to the old man in Midas' garden? Why did Midas help him?
3 What reward did Midas want? Why did he ask for this reward?
4 What happened when Midas' wish was granted?
5 Who did Midas love the most 'of all living things'?
6 What happened to his daughter?
7 What did Midas feel about what happened to his daughter?
8 What did Midas ask Dionysus? Why did he ask him this?
9 Why did Midas have to bathe in the river? What happened?
10 What lesson do you think Midas learnt from what happened?

Thinking about being greedy

Key question: What is greed ?

1 Midas wanted more gold. Have you ever wanted more of something?
2 Have you ever asked for more of something? Give an example.
3 Do you always get what you ask for? Why?
4 Is it good to get everything you ask for? Why, or why not?
5 If people ask you to do something, do you always do it? Why?
6 If people ask you to give them something, do you always give it? Why?
7 What does 'being greedy' mean? Give an example.
8 Do you think everyone is greedy?
9 Is it good to be greedy? Why?
10 What can stop people being greedy?

Further activities

- Ask children to think through their day, imagining and describing what would happen if everything they touched turned to gold.
- Cover some of the words in the story, and see if children can predict the words from the context of the sentence or story.
- Play Hunt the Vowel. See how many words can be found containing a chosen vowel i.e. a, e, i, o, or u.
- Make up a story about a greedy boy or girl (read the poem 'Griselda' by Eleanor Farjeon).
- Display and discuss gold-coloured pictures and objects.

18 The Wind and the Sun

One day the Wind and the Sun had a quarrel. In fact they were always quarrelling, for if the truth were known the Wind was rather jealous of the Sun. Everyone could see the Sun shining like a golden ball in the sky, but no-one could see the Wind. The Wind showed his strength by blowing things about, and he was very proud of all he could do. On the day of this quarrel he met the Sun at the top of a hill, and each began to boast about how clever they were.

'I,' said the Sun, 'bring warmth to the earth. Without me there would be no flowers in the fields or fruit on the trees.'

'And I,' said the Wind, 'can blow the leaves from the trees and make the seas roar.'

'No-one is stronger than I am,' said the Sun as he glowed.

'No-one is stronger than I am,' said the Wind with a roar. Once more they began to quarrel.

Just then a man came walking by. He was wearing a thick overcoat.

'Let us try a try a test of strength,' whispered the Wind, 'and see which of us can make the man take his coat off. As I am stronger than you, I am bound to win.'

'We'll see about that,' grunted the Sun. 'You try first, and I will wait behind this cloud.'

So the Wind blew down upon the man with all his strength. The man pulled the coat around him, so the Wind blew harder, and the man pulled the coat even more tightly around him. The Wind roared and bent the trees. Leaves went swirling in the air. The man's coat tails flapped. The Wind howled down the hill, but still the man kept his coat on. At last the Wind sighed and gave up. 'Its no good,' he puffed. 'It can't be done.'

The Sun came out from behind the cloud. 'Now let me try,' he beamed. Slowly the Sun rose high in the sky and began to shine. The man felt warm, then hot, then hotter still, then the hottest he had felt in all his life. The Sun beat down with all his force. The man started to sweat, and then unbuttoned his coat. Finally when the heat was too much he took off his coat and sat down under the shade of a tree.

'Who do you think is stronger now, Mr Wind?' glowed the Sun. There was no answer, only a gentle rustle of leaves as the Wind blew away.

(Aesop's fable)

Thinking about the story

Key question: What does the story mean?

1 Why did the Wind and the Sun quarrel?
2 The story says the Wind was jealous of the Sun. What does 'jealous' mean?
3 Why was the Wind jealous of the Sun? Was he right to be jealous? Why?
4 Why did the Sun think he was stronger than the Wind?
5 Why did the Wind think he was stronger than the Sun?
6 What test of strength did they decide to do?
7 Do you think it was a fair test? Why?
8 When the Wind tried the test, what happened? Why was this?
9 When the Sun tried the test, what happened? Why was this?
10 What kind of story is this? Does it have a moral?

Thinking about boasting

Key question: What is a boast?

1 The Wind and the Sun quarrelled. Do you ever quarrel with others? Give an example.
2 Can you quarrel with a friend and still be friends?
3 The Wind and the Sun boasted. What did they boast about?
4 What does it mean 'to boast'? Is being 'proud' different from being 'boastful'?
5 Do you ever boast? If not, why not? If so, what about?
6 Is it a good thing to boast? Why, or why not?
7 Have you ever heard people boasting? What do they boast about?
8 Why do people boast?
9 What other reasons are there why people want to boast?
10 What thing are you proudest of? Do you boast about it? Why, or why not?

Further activities

- Imagine this story is a play. Describe the costumes the Sun and the Wind could wear.
- Brainstorm weather words, divide them into nouns/verbs/adjectives and make them into sentences about each kind of weather.
- Draw weather pictures. Write titles for them. Discuss how you know it is windy/hot etc. in each picture.
- Look at newspaper weather reports. What were the hottest/coldest places? Find them in an atlas.
- List the things you are good at. Highlight the three you are proudest of.

19 The Mirror of Truth

The King was once a handsome man. But as the years passed he grew fat and lazy. He had big meals and always ate two of everything he liked. He never walked when he could ride in his carriage. He was a happy man until one day he looked in the mirror.

'Who is that ugly man staring at me in the mirror?' he wondered. 'It's me!' he thought, 'that pale face, those puffy cheeks, those dark bags under the eyes. Quick, change my mirror, I don't like the look of this one at all!' The King tried every mirror in the palace, but in each one he looked the same.

He called for his servant and asked, 'Am I really that ugly?'

The servant thought for a moment, then said to the King, 'Oh no, Your Majesty, there is something wrong with your mirrors. What you need is the Mirror of Truth. My grandmother told me about it. It's magic, for it is the only mirror in which you can see yourself as you really are.'

'Good,' said the King. 'Go and fetch me that mirror.'

'I am afraid it is not as easy as that,' said the servant. 'For the magic to work you must fetch it yourself, Your Majesty.'

'Really?' said the King. 'Oh well, I'll go in my carriage.'

'Ah,' said the servant, 'my grandmother said that you can only find the magic mirror if you fetch it on foot.'

'You mean walking?' said the King. The servant nodded.

'All right,' said the King sadly, 'we will go after I've had a nice big lunch.'

'Ah,' said the servant, 'the magic mirror can only be found very early in the morning when the sun has just risen.'

'But I'm still asleep then,' moaned the King.

'I will wake you, Your Majesty. There are some magic exercises we must do before we set out. Then we are sure to find the Mirror of Truth.'

The next day the servant woke the King at dawn, and showed him the magic exercises, which included touching his toes. The King was surprised. He hadn't seen his toes for many years. Then they went off walking over the hills to find the mirror. But sad to say, they did not find the mirror that day. The next day they did the same. Then the next day, and the next. Still they found no mirror.

For six months they searched. The King by now had become fit and healthy, but he was very disappointed at not finding the mirror. Then early one morning the King saw something shining in the grass. It was a mirror! 'Yes, Your Majesty,' said his servant. 'it must be the Mirror of Truth.'

The King picked it up with trembling fingers and looked into it. What a healthy and handsome face he had. Gone was the pale skin and tired eyes. This must be the Mirror of Truth. The king was happy with what he saw in the mirror, but he was also puzzled. How did the mirror get there? Was the mirror really magic? Why did he look different from how he had looked before? It was a mystery. His servant said nothing, but just looked at the mirror and smiled.

Thinking about the story

Key question: What does the story mean?

1 Why did the king think he was ugly?
2 Why did the servant say the king needed the Mirror of Truth?
3 What according to the servant was the Mirror of Truth?
4 Why was it said to be magic?
5 What did the king have to do to find it?
6 What do you think the 'magic exercises' were?
7 When he found the mirror, what did the king see? Why was this?
8 Where do you think the mirror came from?
9 Do you think it really was a magic mirror? Why?
10 Why did the servant smile? Do you think he knew something the King did not know?

Thinking about keeping fit

Key question: What is keeping fit ?

1 If you eat a lot and do not exercise, like the King in the story, what happens to your body?
2 The King at the start of the story was not fit. What does it mean to be 'fit'?
3 How do you keep fit? What do you do at home/in school that helps you to be fit?
4 Does it matter if you are not fit? Why?
5 Does anyone help you to keep fit?
6 How can you tell if someone is fit and healthy?
7 How can you tell if someone is not fit or not healthy?
8 What sort of people in life need to keep their bodies fit?
9 Can you keep your mind fit? If so, how?
10 Which is more important: keeping your body fit or your mind fit?

Further activities

• Discuss what the King thinks of the servant, and what the servant thinks of the King.
• Find examples of direct speech in the story and show how it is written.
• Brainstorm words to describe the King 'before' and 'after' the story. Draw 'before' and 'after' pictures of the king.
• Record pulse rates before and after exercise. Draw a graph to show the results.
• Investigate surfaces that reflect, such as mirrors, metal, glass, water etc.

20 Seeing the Light

Many years ago in India there lived a King who had two sons. Both boys were tall and strong, and the King wondered which of his two princes would be best to rule the kingdom when he died. They were both skilled with the sword. Each could shoot an arrow and ride a horse.

The King could not make up his mind which of the sons should be chosen. Both were brave and strong, but which of the princes was the wisest? The King decided to give them a test to find out.

Late one evening when the work was done, he sent for the two boys and said to them, 'Tomorrow, my sons, in the early morning before the sun has risen, I want you to go to the market and buy me something that will fill this great hall.' Then he gave each boy a small silver coin.

'This is a test,' said the King, 'to see which of you is wise enough to rule my kingdom when I am gone.' With that he said goodnight, and the boys were left wondering how they could buy something with one small coin that would fill the great hall.

The next morning the princes rose early and made their way to market looking for something to buy. It was crowded even at that early hour, with plenty of things for sale. The first prince looked at the great bags of rice, but a sackful cost more than one coin. He saw piles of fruit, but they too were expensive, and bags of wool, salt, sugar and spice, but one coin would not buy nearly enough to fill his father's hall.

At last, as evening shadows began to fall, he found a stall piled high with straw. 'That will be cheap and light to carry,' he thought. So with the coin he had, he bought as much straw as he could carry. But he found the straw was not nearly enough to fill the hall, it only covered the floor.

When the sun had set his brother returned. He too had spent the day searching the market with his one copper coin, but he had found something that would fill the great hall. It was a candle. He placed it carefully in the middle of the hall and lit it.

The flame from the candle shone through the darkness and filled the great hall with light. When his father saw the light he was pleased. 'You are wise, my son' he said, 'and have shown me you are fit to rule my kingdom.'

(Indian story)

Thinking about the story

Key question: What does the story mean?

1   What was the test the King gave his two boys?
2   Why did he give them this test? What did he want to find out?
3   Where did the boys go? Why did they go there?
4   What sort of things do you think they saw there?
5   What did the first prince decide to buy with his silver coin?
6   Why did he choose that? Was it a sensible thing to choose?
7   What did the second prince buy? What did he do then?
8   Do you think this was a fair test to give to the princes?
9   Do you think the King chose the wiser son? Why?
10 What might happen next in the story?

Thinking about seeing

Key question: What is seeing ?

1   How do we see things?
2   Can you see in the dark?
3   To see things we need light. Where does light come from?
4   What would it be like if you could not see (if you were blind)?
5   Can you see things in your mind?
6   Can you see things in your dreams?
7   Can you see things which are not there?
8   Can you see yourself? How?
9   What things do you know that you cannot see?
10 How do you know something is true if you cannot see it?

Further activities

- Make a story board to show Title/Setting/Problem/Event/Solution/Conclusion (see p 76).
- Discuss punctuation and show how it helps to make sense in reading the story.
- Discuss and chart 'seeing' words e.g. 'see', 'look', 'spy', 'view', 'glimpse', 'stare'.
- Blindfold a child to see if s/he can identify different objects by touch on a tray. Ask others to describe objects to be identified by a blindfolded child.
- Collect pictures of objects or objects that give light e.g. torch, candle, lamp, fairy lights etc.

21 The Cats and the Chapatti

Once upon a time two cats found a chapatti. A chapatti is a kind of Indian bread, a little like a flat pancake. The cats were greedy and began to quarrel over it.

'It's mine!' said one cat. 'I saw it first!'

'No, it's mine,' said the other cat. 'I saw it before you!'

While the cats were arguing, a monkey came by and he looked at the chapatti. He felt hungry and wanted the chapatti for himself.

The monkey thought for a while then said, 'Sisters, why are you quarrelling? To be fair, you should share the chapatti and split it in two. Let me break it in half for you.'

At first the cats were not sure. Was this a fair thing to do?

They soon agreed it was. So the monkey picked up the chapatti and broke it into two pieces. He then held the pieces up for the cats to see.

'Oh dear,' he said, 'look, one piece is larger than the other,' and he broke a bit off the larger piece and ate it. He held the pieces up again.

'Oh dear,' he said, 'they are still not equal,' and he broke off another piece and popped it in his mouth. The two cats watched, not realising what was happening.

Again the monkey held the pieces up and said, 'Oh dear, they are *still* not equal,' and ate another piece off the bigger bit. The clever monkey carried on doing this and the pieces became smaller and smaller. Still the cats could not see his plan.

At last there was only one small piece left. 'Oh dear,' he said, 'it's too small to cut in half,' so he quickly gobbled it up and ran away laughing.

The two cats stared at each other and slowly realised that they had been tricked by the clever monkey.

(Indian folktale)

Thinking about the story

Key question: What does the story mean?

1   How many cats were there? How do you know?
2   What did the cats find?
3   What is a chapatti?
4   Where was the chapatti? Why was it there?
5   Why did the cats quarrel?
6   Why did the monkey want the chapatti?
7   What was the monkey's plan to get the chapatti for himself?
8   When did the cats realise they had been tricked?
9   Do you think the monkey was right when he said the last piece was too small to cut in half?
10 What do you think the moral of this story is?

Thinking about quarrelling

Key question: What is a quarrel?

1   What does it mean to quarrel with someone?
2   Why do people quarrel? What reasons are there for quarrels?
3   How many people are there in a quarrel?
4   Can you quarrel with yourself? Have you ever had a quarrel with yourself?
5   Have you ever had a quarrel with other people? Give an example.
6   Do you only quarrel with someone you don't like?
7   What do you do if your friends start quarrelling?
8   How could you help them end a quarrel?
9   What is the best way of keeping out of quarrels?
10 Is it ever good to have a quarrel? Why, or why not?

Further activities

• Discuss what each character might be thinking at different stages of the story.
• Find out what children know about bread, and write down their sentences or questions.
• Make a class list of words that rhyme with words in the story e.g. cat/sat, fair/share.
• Make up a story about a quarrel.
• Make a chapatti. You need: 100g plain flour, 15g margarine, pinch of salt, some water, some oil or margarine. Mix the flour, margarine and salt together, add enough water to form the mixture into a firm ball, flatten the ball, melt some margarine or oil in a frying pan, and fry the chapatti on both sides.

22 The Gift of Fire

Long ago in the Dreamtime, when many animals were not yet born, there lived a man called Numul. He was the only one who had fire, which he carried with him in a piece of wood. He had to be careful to keep it alive at all times.

Wherever Numul went he took with him the gift of fire. He travelled from one end of the country to the other, and wherever he saw men eating raw food he would make them a fire. He put dry grass on his wood, blew on it, and the fire would flame up. Numul would then show them how to cook their food.

One day a strange creature, half-man and half-fish, came to see Numul to ask for the gift of fire.

'Where do you come from?' asked Numul.

'I come from the sea,' said the Fish Man.

'Then fire is not for you,' said Numul. 'If fire touches water we will lose it forever.'

The Fish Man wanted fire, so he went away to think of a plan to trick Numul. He painted his face and body so that Numul would not recognise him, and waited where he knew Numul would come.

Numul stopped when he saw a man with a painted face and body sitting and eating raw food.

'Look,' said Numul, 'let me make a fire for you and show you how to cook your food.'

'Yes please,' said the painted man. 'If you give me fire you can share my food.'

So Numul made fire and cooked the food, and they ate a large meal. Then Numul lay back to sleep, his precious piece of wood buried in the hot ash of the fire. As Numul lay sleeping the Fish Man grabbed the piece of wood and rushed to the sea. As he ran the wind blew the wood and it began to burn. When Numul awoke from his sleep he saw the light of his fire disappearing in the darkness.

The Fish Man waded into the water holding the fire above him. Numul raced after him. The Fish Man disappeared under the waves, and just as the fire was going underwater Numul grabbed it. The fire stick looked dead, but when Numul held it in the air the wind lit the flame.

'We nearly lost fire forever,' thought Numul. 'I must think of a way of leaving my gift so that all can share it.'

Taking his fire-stick, Numul went on a walk through the bush. Whenever he came to a tree he stopped, then hit the burning stick against it so that sparks flew high into the branches and were hidden there.

As it was then and so it is now. When someone wants to make a fire they only have to rub two dry sticks together for fire to come out of the tree again.

That is how Numul brought the gift of fire for us all to share.

(Dreamtime story from the Aborigines of Australia)

Thinking about the story

Key question: What does the story mean?

1   When did Numul live?
2   What was special about Numul?
3   What did Numul do with his fire stick? Why did he do this?
4   What strange creature came to see Numul? What did he want?
5   Why did Numul not give him fire?
6   What was the Fish Man's plan to try to trick Numul?
7   Did the Fish Man's plan work? Why?
8   How did Numul share the gift of fire? Why did he do this?
9   Do you think this could be a true story? Why, or why not?
10 Why do you think the Aborigines of Australia tell this story?

Thinking about gifts

Key question: What is a gift?

1   This story is called The Gift of Fire. What is a gift?
2   What is your favourite thing that you have been given?
3   Are there special times for giving and receiving presents?
4   Why do people give gifts or presents? Have you given any gifts to others?
5   Do you know any stories about giving gifts?
6   What makes something a *good* gift for someone?
7   If someone gives you something, is there anything you should do or say in return?
8   Some people say we all have gifts from God or from nature. What gifts are these?
9   If you could give one gift to a young baby, what would it be?
10 Is it better to give a gift or to receive a gift?

Further activities

* Ask children to close their eyes, imagine and then describe what the characters in the story look like.
* Make up a list of questions you would want to ask Numul or the Fish Man.
* Collect words associated with fire to place around a picture of fire (write them with charcoal).
* Look at a flame. Write a fire poem, using the display of words about fire to help.
* Discuss the dangers of fire (e.g. playing with matches), fire precautions and fire drill.

23 The Discontented Pig

There was once a pig who lived on his own in a small cottage near a village. In his garden he planted seeds and grew juicy vegetables and beautiful flowers. People came from miles around to buy what he grew. He won prizes for his plants and flowers. Every day the pig could be seen digging, planting or weeding his garden. He was a very good gardener.

After some years the pig grew tired of all the hard work involved in growing vegetables. 'There must be easier work to do,' he said. 'I think I'll go and find a better job.' So off he went.

Soon he came to a cottage where he heard the sound of sweet music. It was a cat playing the violin. 'If a cat can play the fiddle then so can I,' thought the pig. 'Playing music must be easier than digging a garden.' So the pig asked the cat, 'Will you teach me to play?'

'Of course,' said the cat. 'All you need is to practise five hours a day for the next few years and you'll become good at the violin.'

'Five hours a day!' said the pig. 'I don't think I'll bother, thank you. Goodbye.'

Next he came to the house of a dog who made cheese. There was the dog stirring a large bucket of milk.

'Will you show me how to make cheese?' asked the pig. 'I am sure it is easier than my job.'

'Certainly,' said the dog. 'Take this spoon and stir as fast as you can until the cheese is formed.'

The pig took the spoon and began to stir. After a while his arms were aching and he stopped for a rest. 'You mustn't stop,' said the dog, 'or you will spoil the cheese.'

'My arms are dropping off!' said the pig. 'Goodbye!'

Next he saw a beekeeper taking honey out of his beehives. 'I'm sure being a beekeeper is easier than my job,' said the pig. 'Will you teach me to be a bee-keeper?'

'Of course,' said the beekeeper. 'Just take out that honeycomb from the beehive.' The pig bent down and carefully picked up the honeycomb. At once several bees flew out and stung him on the face. The pig screamed with pain and ran away.

'Come back!' shouted the man. 'If you want to be a beekeeper you must put up with a few stings.'

'No thanks!' said the pig, and he ran back home as fast as his legs would carry him. Soon he was busy again working in his own garden. And he felt really happy again to be working in his own garden.

Thinking about the story

Key question: What does the story mean?

1   Where did the pig live?

2   What work did the pig do?

3   Why did he think it was such hard work?

4   What did he decide to do?

5   What happened when he met the cat who played the violin?

6   What happened when he met the dog?

7   What happened when he met the beekeeper?

8   Why did the pig run home?

9   Why was he happy being back in his own garden?

10 Which kind of work in the story do you think is the hardest (and easiest)?

Thinking about work

Key question: What is work?

1   What is work? Can you give me an example?

2   What is play?

3   Is work the same as play? What is the difference?

4   Does everyone have work to do? Who does (or doesn't) have to work?

5   What work needs doing at home? Who does it? Why?

6   What jobs need to be done at school? Who does them? Why?

7   What work do you have to do? What work are you best at? Why?

8   'All work and no play makes Jack a dull boy.' What does this saying mean?

9   Is it a good thing to work hard? Why?

10 What helps you to work hard?

Further activities

- Invite children to act out the story while you read it. Do it again, adding sound effects.

- Find out what jobs the children would like to do. Write a letter of application saying what job you would like and why you would be good at it.

- Do a mind map of words to do with work e.g. jobs at home, jobs at school or jobs in the world. How many words about work can you find?

- Discuss work that needs to be done, decide who will do it and how they can be helped.

- Cultivate a garden e.g. plant seeds or make a miniature garden in a tray or box.

24 The Shirt of Happiness

There was once a very grumpy king. Nothing ever seemed to be right for him. He grumbled when he got up in the morning, because it was either too early or too late. He moaned about his food, because there was either too much or too little. He complained about the weather, because it was either too hot or too cold. He found something wrong with everything. He was a very grumpy king.

One day he called all his ministers together and said: 'I feel so unhappy. Can any of you suggest a solution to my problem?'

The ministers shook their heads, then the oldest one spoke. 'Your Majesty,' he said, 'there is only one way to cure your problem. You must find the Shirt of Happiness and wear it. No one knows what the shirt looks like, only that it is worn by a truly happy man.'

'Very well,' said the king. 'Each of you must search my kingdom until you find this truly happy man. When you have found him, bring me his shirt so that I can wear it.' So the ministers went off to search for the Shirt of Happiness. But nowhere, in the country or the town, could they find a truly happy man.

At last they found a man who was truly happy. But this man was so poor that he did not have a shirt. So what were the ministers to say to the king? The oldest minister thought hard and had an idea.

When the king asked if anyone had found the Shirt of Happiness, the old minister replied 'Yes, here it is!' He then handed the king an old white shirt. The king put it on, and it fitted perfectly. The ministers all smiled, and the king smiled too. He wore his special shirt every day and felt happy. 'Today,' he would say, 'I am going to put on my Happy Shirt.' And as he put it on a smile spread across his face. Never had he felt better or enjoyed himself more. The Shirt of Happiness really seemed to work.

A few days later the King noticed that one of his old shirts was missing from the royal wardrobe. Now he had his Shirt of Happiness you would not think he would miss one of his old shirts. But it set him thinking ... and he sent for his old minister.

The king asked where the Shirt of Happiness had come from and the old minister told the true story. He had taken one of the king's own shirts and pretended it was the Shirt of Happiness. At first the king was very angry, but then he laughed. That old shirt had taught him a lesson - it was much more fun to be happy than to be unhappy.

'From today,' said the king, 'I shall make every shirt I wear a Shirt of Happiness.'

Thinking about the story

Key question: What does the story mean?

1   Why was the king unhappy?
2   What makes people unhappy?
3   The king had ministers to help him. What is a minister?
4   What advice would you give the king if you were his minister?
5   How did the old minister know about the Shirt of Happiness?
6   Why did the king feel happy when he put on the shirt?
7   What lesson had the king learnt at the end of the story?
8   Could a shirt make a king happy? Why or why not?
9   What do you think he felt and did when he was happy?
10 Do you think the king was happy ever after? Why, or why not?

Thinking about Happiness

Key question: What does it mean to be happy ?

1   Are you happy? Why (or why not)?
2   What do you feel like when you are happy?
3   Is it a good thing to be happy? Why?
4   Can you say one thing that makes you feel happy, or unhappy?
5   Can you be happy all the time?
6   Can you tell if someone is happy? If so, how?
7   Can you tell if someone is unhappy (or sad)? If so, how?
8   Can you be happy and unhappy (or sad) at the same time?
9   What can you say or do to make someone feel happy?
10 Can you make yourself feel happy? If so, how?

Further Activities

- Act out a scene between the king and his court before and after the story.
- Finish this sentence: 'Happiness is ...' Make this the first line of a list poem.
- Brainstorm words linked to the central word 'Happiness', and discuss synonyms.
- Design your own Shirt of Happiness. What colours, shapes or words would it have?
- List the five senses, and discuss, write or draw what makes you happy e.g. 'A smell which makes me happy is ... because ...'.

25 Feeling the Elephant

One day a merchant was about to set out on a trip when he had an idea.

'I will take an elephant with me,' he thought. 'The Arabs have never seen an elephant. They are a curious people. They will pay me well to see a real live elephant.'

So the merchant bought himself an elephant and took it with him on his journey to the Arab lands.

After much travel the merchant came to an Arab town. When it was dark and he was sure that no one would see, he led the elephant into the city. Once there he shut the elephant in a large dark house, and waited until the next morning.

When the sun rose people were surprised to see a notice pinned up outside the house: 'Hurry, hurry, come and see a real live elephant, here for one day only.' People began waiting outside the door, and soon a crowd began to gather. They had never seen an elephant before, and they were very excited.

'What did an elephant look like? Was it that animal with a horn on its head? Would it bite?'

At 9 o'clock the merchant opened the door and said, 'There is only room for one at a time.' The first man paid his money and went in.

Inside the room it was pitch dark. The man could not see a thing. He put out his hand and felt something. It was the elephant! He moved his hand up the elephant's trunk and then down again. When he came out his friends crowded round him. 'What was it like?' they asked.

'It was just like a long fat snake,' said the man.

The second person went in to feel the elephant. When he reached out he felt the rough skin of the elephant's ear. He walked round the room, reached out, and felt the other ear. When he came out, the crowd asked what the elephant was like.

'It had wings,' said the man.

'Nonsense,' said the first man. 'It was like a snake!'

A third man went into the dark room. His hand touched the leg of the elephant. He felt carefully up and down, then came out to tell the others, 'It's tall and straight like the trunk of a tree.'

'No, it's long and floppy like a snake,' said the first man.

'It's like a bird!' said the second man. Soon they were involved in a great argument. A fourth man went in and he felt along the elephant's back.

'You can sit on it,' he said. 'It's just like a big sofa.' The arguments went on. 'It's like a snake!' 'No, it's like a bird!' 'It's like a tree!' 'It's like a sofa!' Each one had felt the elephant, and they each had part of the truth. Only one man knew the whole truth, and he wasn't telling anybody.

(Persian story)

Thinking about the story

Key question: What does the story mean?

1   What is a merchant? Why does he travel?
2   What did he take with him? Why did he take it? Where did he take it?
3   Why did he wait until dark to enter the city?
4   What did the first man feel? What did he think?
5   What did the second man feel? What did he think?
6   What did the third man feel? What did he think?
7   What did the fourth man feel? What did he think?
8   Why did each of them know only part of the truth?
9   Why did the merchant not tell them about the elephant?
10   Do you think this is a true story? Why, or why not?

Thinking about knowing

Key question: What is knowing and believing?

1   The men did not know what an elephant was. Why was this?
2   Can you give an example of something you do not know?
3   Can you think of something that I don't know?
4   Can you give an example of something nobody knows?
5   Do adults know more than children? Why?
6   Do you know something that nobody knows?
7   Is it possible to know everything? Why, or why not?
8   Is there a difference between knowing something and believing it?
9   What are the most important things you should know?
10   If you don't know something, what can you do to find out?

Further activities

- Ask children to retell the story from the point of view of one of the characters.
- Create a list of questions about elephants. Use reference books to try to find answers to the questions.
- Brainstorm words to describe an elephant, and parts of an elephant (e.g. trunk, ears, skin, tail, size, colour etc.).
- Create a 'feely bag' or box, containing objects for children to feel, describe and identify.
- Ask a child to describe a mystery object only they can see. The others try to draw what is being described, before the object is revealed.

26 The Man who Sold his Shadow

There was once a young man named John who was always grumbling. He wanted more than anything to be rich and famous. One day his wish came true, and this is how it happened.

It was a hot sunny day and the sun was making long shadows everywhere. John was walking along a street when he was stopped by a merchant.

'You have a fine shadow there, young man,' said the merchant.

'Yes, my shadow always comes when the sun shines,' said John.

'I am buying shadows,' said the merchant. 'May I buy yours?'

'What will you give me for it?' asked John.

'If you give me your shadow I promise to make you rich and famous,' said the merchant. So John quickly agreed.

The merchant took a pair of scissors out of his pocket and bent down. Snip! Snip! He cut off John's shadow close at his heels, rolled it up and stuffed it in his bag. Then with a funny sort of laugh he raised his hat and walked away.

From that day on John's luck seemed to change. He became rich and well known throughout the land. John's friends began to envy his fame and money.

Then people began to notice something strange about John. 'Look!' they said. 'The sun is shining, yet John has got no shadow. How can that be?' They began to point at John whenever they saw him, and whisper among themselves.

John began to notice how people avoided him, and stood staring at where his shadow should be. Poor John began to miss his shadow. He would jump quickly round to see if it was there. But no, even in bright sunshine he had no shadow.

John began to stay indoors when the sun was shining so that people would not see him. Even when it was dull and cloudy he was frightened to go out in case he was seen. At last he was so miserable that he went to the merchant and begged to have his shadow back.

'All right,' said the merchant, 'but only if you give me all the riches you have gained.'

John agreed, and he got his shadow back. From that day on he never grumbled so much, for he knew that a happy life is made up of shadows as well as sunshine.

Thinking about the story

Key question: What does the story mean?

1 The story says John was always grumbling. What do you think he grumbled about?
2 What did John want to be? Why did he want this?
3 What did the merchant want?
4 Why did John let him have his shadow?
5 What did the merchant do with John's shadow?
6 Why do you think the merchant gave 'a funny sort of laugh'?
7 What does it mean when someone's luck has changed?
8 How might John have become rich?
9 Why did John become so miserable?
10 What does it mean, 'a happy life is made up of shadows as well as sunshine'?

Thinking about grumbling

Key question: Why do people grumble?

1 What does it mean, to grumble?
2 What do people grumble about? (The weather, work, traffic, noise, other people?)
3 What do you grumble about?
4 What do your family grumble about at home?
5 What do your friends grumble about?
6 If you grumble, does it mean you are unhappy?
7 Does it help to grumble?
8 People sometimes complain when things go wrong. What does it mean to complain?
9 Have you any complaints about school?
10 What could be done about the complaints people have?

Further activities

- Act or mime the story as it is retold.
- Identify punctuation, and show how it helps in reading the story aloud with intonation and expression.
- Explore antonyms like light/dark, love/hate, rich/poor, happy/unhappy, indoors/outdoors, long/short etc.
- Make silhouette pictures of children (e.g. use a bright light, draw the outline of their profile then colour it in) or shadow puppets.
- Study shadows at different times of the day, and the use of sundials.

27 Why the Spider Lives in a Web

There was a time when all the animals liked the Spider, but Spider's special friends were Tiger and Monkey. This was funny, for they were big and Spider was small, they liked to work and Spider did not, they did not steal but Spider did.

Tiger and Monkey had three fields. They grew yams in one field, bananas in the second, and sweetcorn in the third. Spider used to sit and watch while his friends worked. When the yams were ready, Tiger and Monkey went to dig them up. To their surprise they found that some had been taken. So they set a trap for the thief. The next day they went to the field they saw someone in the trap. It was Spider!

'Please let me go,' said Spider. 'I will never take your yams again.' So they let him go.

When the bananas were ready for picking, Tiger and Monkey took their baskets into the field. But they found that some of their bananas were missing. So Monkey said he would keep watch that night and try to catch the thief. Sure enough, as Monkey sat in the dark, he saw someone climbing the banana trees. Monkey ran across the field and caught hold of the thief. It was Spider.

'Oh, please let me go,' said Spider. 'I will never steal again.' This time they beat him and let him go.

Then Monkey and Tiger went into their third field to pick their corn. But somebody had been there before them, for some of the corn was missing. Tiger and Monkey guessed who it was, and kept watch for Spider. The next night Spider went into the field of corn. Tiger and Monkey crept after him. Spider did not know they were there, and happily began to pick the corn. When he looked round he saw Monkey and Tiger.

Spider ran as fast as he could and after him ran Tiger and Monkey. They chased through the forest. As he rushed past a banana tree Spider tore off a thin, strong thread. He rushed to an orange tree and tied an end round a branch. From this he swung to another tree and the thread made a bridge. When Tiger climbed one tree, Spider swung across to another. When Monkey climbed that tree, Spider ran to the middle of his bridge between the trees and sat there.

Spider was safe. But what could he eat, hanging high up on his thread? Spider was a clever fellow, so he found a way to get food. He spun a web to catch flies to eat, and he has been doing the same thing ever since.

(West Indian story)

Thinking about the story

Key question: What does the story mean?

1   All the animals liked Spider, but who were his special friends?
2   At first all the animals liked Spider. Why do you think they liked him?
3   How was Spider different from his friends?
4   What did Tiger and Monkey grow in their fields?
5   What happened when Spider tried to steal the yams?
6   How might he have been trapped?
7   What happened each time he was caught stealing?
8   How did Spider escape when Tiger and Monkey chased him?
9   Do you think Spider would rather have lived in his web or stayed with his friends? Why?
10 What kind of story is it? What does it try to explain?

Thinking about stealing

Key question: What is stealing?

1   Spider took what Tiger and Monkey grew. Was that stealing?
2   What does it mean 'to steal something'? What is a thief?
3   Is it right to steal from your friends?
4   Is it right to steal from anyone?
5   Has someone ever stolen something from you? Give an example.
6   Have you ever been tempted to steal something? When were you tempted?
7   What kind of people steal things?
8   What should happen to people who get caught stealing?
9   If you find something and keep it, is that the same as stealing?
10 Is right or wrong to steal things? Why?

Further activities

- Ask children to retell the story from the point of view of each of the characters in the story.
- Ask children to identify and match upper case letters on the page with lower case letters.
- Brainstorm words to do with spiders for children to use in their own writing.
- Study spiral shapes and animation of spiders spinning a web on a CD Rom encyclopedia. Draw spiders' webs (or make them with black thread).
- Make spider models e.g. out of cup sections of eggboxes and pipe cleaners, painted and decorated.

28 Mary and her Bones

Many years ago there was a girl called Mary Anning who lived in the seaside town of Lyme Regis in Dorset. She had no mother or father, and she made her living by selling sea shells she found by the sea shore. She was good at collecting shells, and many of the shells she found were very beautiful.

Each day Mary would climb over the rocks on the seashore with her basket in one hand and a hammer in the other. Here and there she would tap a rock with her hammer, and look at the broken pieces very carefully to see if she could find a hidden shell. When she saw a shell she would put it into her basket, ready to sell to the visitors who came to the town in the summer.

One day Mary found something very strange in the rocks. They looked like the bones of a fish, but it was bigger than any fish Mary had ever seen. It was different too, for this fish had flippers instead of fins on each side of its body.

She asked some workmen to help dig the rock out for her. A man named Mr Henley gave Mary £23 for the bones, which was a lot of money in those days. He said Mary had found something very important. The bones were the skeleton of a prehistoric monster, a kind of dinosaur called Ichthyosaurus, which means 'fish lizard'.

Mary found many other bones by the seashore. All were bones of dinosaurs which had lived there millions of years ago. One of the skeletons she found was a 'flying lizard' called Pterodactyl. Although it had wings it was not a bird. It had teeth and wings made of leathery skin. People came from all over the world to see the bones Mary had found. She became famous, and many of the bones she found can be seen in museums today.

When Mary died a beautiful window was put into her local church at Lyme Regis to remind people of how she helped us to know more about prehistoric monsters, and how it started when she was a little girl looking for shells on the sea shore.

(True story)

Thinking about the story

Key question: What does the story mean?

1   Where did Mary live?
2   Why did she collect shells?
3   How did she find them?
4   What was the strange thing she found in the rocks?
5   How did she get the bones she found in the rock?
6   What did Mr Henley give Mary for the bones?
7   How did they know they were the bones of a prehistoric monster?
8   Do you know the names of any dinosaurs? What were the dinosaurs in the story?
9   Where might you see the bones that Mary found?
10 What did they do to remind people about Mary? Why did they do this?

Thinking about finding out

Key question: If we don't know, how do we find out ?

1   Mary found things on the sea shore. What have you found on a sea shore?
2   What kinds of things can you find on a sea shore?
3   If you found a shell and wanted to know its name, how could you find out?
4   If you had a shell and couldn't find its name, who could you ask?
5   Could there be a shell which no-one has ever seen or found before?
6   The bones that Mary found can be seen in museums. What are museums for?
7   How can a computer help you find things out?
8   If dinosaurs lived millions of years ago, how do we know what they look like?
9   Are there things about the world that we don't know? What don't we know?
10 If you don't know something, how can you try to find out?

Further activities

* Retell the story as a TV news report by being interviewed in role as Mary.
* Find and write down information on dinosaurs from reference books or CD Roms.
* Use a dictionary to find words with prefix 'pre-'.
* Make a model of a dinosaur, or a mobile of flying creatures, or 'pretend' fossil out of plaster.
* Study and draw fossils, dinosaur footprints or skeletons (life size if possible).

Note: see also the story of Columba and the Loch Ness monster, p 74.

29 The Parts of the Body

A body is made up of many parts, and they all work together, but it was not always so. Once long ago the parts of the body did not work well together at all. Each part had a will and a voice of its own.

One day the parts of the body began to find fault with the stomach. 'What does he do all day?' said the hands. 'We work for our living, but he's lazy, he just lies there while we give him things to eat.'

'Quite true, ' said the feet. 'He does nothing, while we have to walk miles carrying his great weight around.'

'What about us?' said the teeth. 'We are worn out with chewing food, just so that he can feel contented.'

'We have had enough,' said the hands.

'So have we,' stamped the feet.

'And us,' snapped the teeth.

The other parts of the body agreed, and they all decided that they would have nothing more to do with the stomach. The feet would not walk the stomach anywhere, the hands would not carry food to the mouth, the mouth would not take food in, the teeth would not chew it. Each part of the body agreed to have nothing to do with the stomach.

They had not been doing this for long before they began to felt very weak. The feet dragged slowly along the ground, the hands could hardly hold a pen and the teeth felt loose in the gums. 'What's wrong? What's wrong?' they all asked.

'I can tell you, my friends, ' grumbled the stomach, who by this time was feeling very sad and hungry. 'It is true I can do nothing without you. But how do you feel without me? The fact is that we can not manage without the help of each other. We only feel good if we work together.'

From that time on the parts of the body have worked together very well, but every now and then you will notice that one of the parts of the body will have a grumble, just to let the body know it has not completely forgotten the quarrel.

Thinking about the story

Key question: What does the story mean?

1 A body is made of many parts. What are the main parts of the body?

2 Why in the story does it say that the parts of the body did not work well together?

3 The story says each part had 'a will and a voice of its own'. What is a 'will'?

4 Why did the other parts of the body grumble about the stomach?

5 What did the hands think? What did the feet think? What did the teeth think?

6 What did the parts of the body agree to do?

7 After a while how did the parts of the body feel?

8 What did the stomach say to the other parts of the body?

9 The body works together now, but sometimes parts grumble. Why is this?

10 Do you think there is a moral or lesson in this story?

Thinking about working together

Key question: Why is it important to work together ?

1 Do the parts of your body work well together? Why?

2 If you have a pain, is your body telling you something?

3 Is one part of your body more important, or are all the parts equally important?

4 Are people in a family, or school, like the parts of a body? Why?

5 Do people always work well together? Why?

6 Is it important for a family or class to work well together. Why?

7 What is a 'team'? What teams do you know of?

8 Are you a member of any team? Which team(s)? What makes you a member?

9 Some teams are called 'United'. Do you know a team called 'United'? What does 'United' mean?

10 Do you prefer to work together with others, or by yourself? Why?

Further activities

- Act the story with children taking different parts, using props and appropriate sounds.

- Each child completes a sentence about a part of their body e.g. 'My hands ...',00 'My feet ...' to make a list poem.

- Label different parts of the body on a large picture. Discuss what each part does.

- Play games that require group co-operation, or make a mural to which everyone contributes.

- Show how easy it is to break one stick, but very hard to break many tied together. Discuss other symbols of united strength e.g. pages of a book, bricks in a wall etc.

30 St Columba and the Loch Ness Monster

In Scotland there is a huge lake called Loch Ness. It is very beautiful, but its waters are dark and mysterious. It is also very deep, well over three hundred metres at its deepest part. Many strange stories have been told about the lake. Here is one of them.

About fourteen hundred years ago St Columba came to Scotland, where he travelled around trying to make the wild Scottish people into Christians. One day he came to the side of Loch Ness. There he expected to find a boat waiting, but instead found some men digging a grave. 'Who is that grave for?' he asked.

'For someone who is dead,' came the answer.

'How did he die?'

'He died from the bite of the monster who lives in these waters - the monster that swims like a whale and bites like the devil!'

'Nonsense!' said Columba. 'There is no such thing.'

There was a boat on the other side of the lake, so the saint ordered one of his men, named Lugue, to swim across the water to fetch the boat.

'Wha... what about the monster?' asked Lugue.

'Have faith,' said Columba. 'Nothing will harm you.'

So Lugue waded in and started swimming. When he was about half way across he got the fright of his life. There was a terrible noise in the water. Suddenly the long neck of the monster rose up, with a gaping mouth and two staring eyes. It drew back its head and darted at Lugue. Lugue's arms and legs turned to jelly.

The onlookers were terrified. But the saint was not afraid.

'Leave that man alone!' he shouted. 'Go back to where you belong!'

At once the beast obeyed and sank slowly beneath the waves. Lugue swam to the shore, still shivering.

'There wa.... was a monster!' he cried.

'Nonsense!' said Columba. 'There is no such thing.'

And from that day to this no one has been harmed by the monster of Loch Ness.

(Scottish legend)

Thinking about the story

Key question: What does the story mean?

1   What is Loch Ness? What does it look like?

2   Why was St Columba in Scotland?

3   When he arrived at Loch Ness, what did Columba expect to find?

4   What did he find men doing on the banks of the Loch? Why?

5   What did the men think the monster looked like?

6   What was Lugue asked to do? What did Lugue think? What did Columba say?

7   While swimming, Lugue got the fright of his life. Why? What happened?

8   Why was Columba not afraid of the monster?

9   Do you think there really was a monster? Why?

10   The story is a legend. What is a legend?

Thinking about real and imaginary things

Key question: What is imagination ?

1   Could there be a real monster in Loch Ness? Why could/couldn't there?

2   Could there be no Loch Ness monster? Could people have imagined it? How?

3   Can you imagine a monster that is not real? If so, can you describe it?

4   Can you imagine something that is not real but could be real? (A 5-legged chair?)

5   Can you imagine something that could never exist? (A 5-legged person?)

6   Do you think other people imagine the same things as you?

7   Can people see things that are not really there?

8   Can people see the same thing and disagree about what they see?

9   How do you know if something is real?

10   Can something be real if you have never seen it? Give an example.

Further activities

- Plot the story out on a map showing Loch Ness.

- Write the story as if it was a news story. What headline (title) would you give the story?

- Brainstorm words to describe the monster.

- Do the story in cartoon form, children each drawing a different cartoon frame.

- Each child draws a monster, and describes it (without others seeing it). Can the others imagine or draw it from the description?

Appendices

APPENDIX 1: How to plot a story

Aim

To help children to outline the plot of a story, using words or pictures to make their own version, a wall display or class book.

Activities

Discuss the main elements of a plot from a story. Show how to record the main events in a frame such as those below with the whole class or group, before asking children to do it in pairs or by themselves.

1   A simple format to write or draw and caption the main events:

Beginning   Middle   End

2   Show events in cartoon format on a sheet of A4 paper:

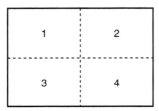

3   Create a story ladder from one sheet, or many sheets, of paper to create a class book or wall display:

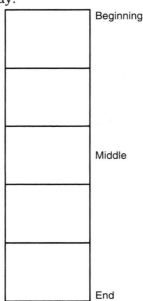

Beginning

Middle

End

APPENDIX 2: How to make a simple eight page book

Aim

To involve the children in the entire process of creating a book – designing, making, writing and illustrating.

Activities

Make a simple eight page book out of one sheet of A4 paper as follows:

1   Fold your paper as shown and openout flat in a landscape position.

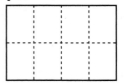

2   Fold in half and cut from the fold to the first crease.

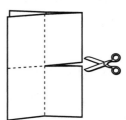

3   Open out and fold in half (landscape).

4   Push the ends to form a cube

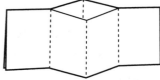

5   Push the ends together to flatten the cube, then fold the pages around to form the book

Two pages are always used for the cover, leaving six pages for the story and illustrations, two pages for the beginning, two for the middle and two for the end of the story.